Iowa Trout Streams

How to Find Them • How to Fish Them

A Guide for Flyfishers
by Jene Hughes

Published by
Second Avenue Bait House
133 Franklin Avenue
Des Moines, Iowa 50314
Telephone 515-282-4217

Printed in the United States of America

2 3 4 5 6 7 8 9 10

ISBN 0-9646375-0-2

To Mary,
who started this book
decades ago by allowing
her 10-year-old son to
commandeer her fly rod.

PHOTO CREDITS
DAVID LEWIS:
FRONT AND BACK COVERS,
PAGES 4 AND 74
JENE HUGHES:
ALL OTHER PHOTOS

COVER DESIGN:
CHARLES G. OLDHAM

Contents

Part I
Iowa Trout Fishing

Part II
The Streams

Part III
Reflections

Foreword

It worked out that I got to spend a few days
fishing with Jene Hughes while he was in the middle of writing this book. He lured me away from my seacoast island in
Maine (home of landlocked salmon and trophy brookies of
legend) with the rash assurance that he'd put me onto some
rising trout that I could cast dry flies to...and probably
catch. And although I've known Jene for many years, and
have found that he usually knows exactly what he's talking
about, still there were doubts: Trout in Iowa? Guaranteed?

My friend Mike and I met Jene in Des Moines, staying just long enough for me to fax a column to my editor
back east and get ready to go fishing. Preparations included
casting practice with the shorter, lighter rods we were to
use, and other essentials like going out to shoot some pool
and hear a jazz band. Within 36 hours we were headed
northeast in search of trout.

We found trout all right, lots of them, browns and
rainbows, indeed rising to my flies. And it wasn't only that
there were trout. There was always more for Jene to show

us about casting, knot-tying, reading the water and landing fish.

There was also a lot of driving around, referring to a thick stack of maps, looking for unmarked turnoffs and obscure landmarks. Jene was, after all, working a good bit of the time, researching this book and acting as our guide. He was obviously intent on gathering accurate information for you, the reader.

One morning is likely to remain vivid in my memory for as long as anything else does. The three of us had walked through the drying corn, along the pasture, and down to a beaver dam at the end of a long, wide pool. With Jene coaching from the bank, I'd caught a couple of nice browns there the previous evening, and this cloudy and damp morning it was Mike's turn.

Jene and I watched as Mike crept down the bank and began false casting toward the familiar patterns of expanding concentric circles. After a while it became obvious that Mike, for one reason or another, just wasn't putting his fly where it needed to be to attract the fish, which nonetheless kept rising regularly.

Abruptly Jene said, "Give me the rod," and slid down the bank to join Mike. He gathered the line, organized himself briefly, made a single false cast, and let the line shoot toward the fish as it rose again. The leader settled on the water gently, the trout slurped up the fly, and the fight was on....but the expression on Mike's face is what lingers in my mind, just as clear as any photograph.

After the fish was released, Jene handed the rod back and we advanced up the pool to undisturbed water. Mike again crept down the bank as we watched another fish begin rising. This time Mike waited, timed the rise, false cast once, and shot the line out like a pro. The strike was violent and the fish was a big one. My face was beginning to hurt from grinning.

The point is this: for a guide to take the rod from his client and catch a fish right in front of him, in effect "showing him up," if you will...would under almost any circumstances be considered unprofessional. But not this time. Jene had met Mike three days earlier, traveled with him, listened to jazz and talked about literature with him, sat alongside him pumping quarters into a slot machine, and in general done a pretty good job of sizing him up. And had calculated that a quick demonstration of how to focus oneself on an early morning rising trout might be just what this guy from Maine needed at that precise moment. Calculated correctly, I should add.

That same kind of calculation has gone into this book. Clearly, it's not just about maps, gravel roads, and spring-fed creeks, although they are a part of it. It's about a much bigger picture, one that includes considerations of the trout's nature, the angler's skills and temperament, and becoming so fully involved in the sport of flyfishing that for a time one can forget everything else entirely. And that, I believe, is a benefit that's darned hard to come by in any other way.

So read this book carefully and take it with you often. I know Jene won't mind if it stays folded open to a map on the dash of your truck for a few days...maybe getting a little dog-eared and gathering dust while you're fishing....

David Lewis
Islesboro, Maine
November 4, 1994

Acknowledgements

When a voice from the lowest bunk rose out of the darkness to ask, "Hey Jene, wouldn't you like to live out here for a year and write a book about the streams?" I answered, "No. I'd like to take a year at home and write a book about those streams. The voice belonged to Iowan Byron Haugh, who was putting me up in a friend's cabin on Idaho's Henry's Fork. A few weeks later I gave Byron an "assignment" to fish Bloody Run so we could compare notes as I worked on the manuscript for this project.

Accompanying me on that trip was Ron Fredrickson, my regular fishing buddy who first showed, and is still showing me, new spots and ways to fish the streams I call the Northern Triangle (Chapter 9). Ron is the most enthusiastic fan of Iowa streams I know (and he blends a wicked color of Hare's Ear dubbing for the northern streams).

Pitching in with fishing information, suggestions, and the use of some of his computer equipment was John Pursell, who started flyfishing at the first clinic I held in

Iowa. He caught his first trout at Richmond Springs just a week or so after that clinic, and I think I was more pleased even than he.

And finally, a large portion of what I know and am presenting here can, directly or indirectly, be traced back to a single angler -- David Halblom. Dave, one of the founding members of the Hawkeye Fly Fishing Association, is a manufacturers' representative in the fly tackle industry, teaches tying at the masters level, is active in the Federation of Fly Fishers (FFF), and even finds time to fish. When he does fish it is with skill and precision that you rarely see on the streams. Any flaws or arguable points herein are definitely my doing, not the result of Dave's influence.

These friends, along with countless visitors to my fly shop who are kind enough to report the results of their fishing excursions, have made it possible for me to gather enough information to assemble this book. I thank all of you.

Part I

Iowa Trout Fishing

Introduction

This is a book that happens to contain several maps. It is not an atlas. My purpose in these pages is to help new fly anglers (and experienced anglers new to Iowa) eliminate some of the hardships that others of us have experienced. My first trip to Northeast Iowa was a total failure. When I got back to Des Moines I wasn't sure I had once cast a fly over a trout. The information in these pages is my attempt to see that other sincere fly anglers get off to a better start.

Toward that end I am including as much general fly fishing information as I think might be useful, even though there is an abundance of fly fishing literature available in other books. If there is nothing totally new for you here, possibly my suggestions will show you a new viewpoint from which to examine aspects of angling that can enhance your success on Iowa streams.

If there is a prejudice it might show up in my preference for either dry flies or classic wet flies fished in the film, which is simply a preference and nothing more.

While I was working on Part II, I assumed that readers would have read and digested the material in Part I, which pertains to all streams. For example, I don't repeat the fact that scuds (fresh water shrimp) and watercress go hand-in-hand every time I mention watercress in a stream.

The map of Spring Branch Creek I have annotated elaborately because beginning fly anglers need a place where they can be successful quickly. Also, the stream is so widely known that there are no "secret spots," and even if there were, the regulations protecting the stream reassure me that divulging the good holes won't fill someone's freezer at the expense of quality sport fishing for others.

The other maps are included simply to show you how to get to the streams and find fishable water with a minimum of frustration. The few fishing spots indicated are the more visible, already popular holes. If you are reading this book to learn "hot spots," you will be disappointed. The maps are solely to help you get your feet on the ground (in the water, actually). Learning the streams is up to you, and in my opinion that is one of the true joys of Iowa fishing. Carrying that philosophy one step further can lead you to finding a favorite stream that is not even discussed here. Like most places, 90 percent of Iowa trout fishing is done on 10 percent of the water.

I saw a poster recently for a motorcycle club rally that held a sage piece of advice: "Leave your attitudes at home." That sentiment could be expressed in more refined prose, but it could not be more true. If you set out with reservations about the quality of Iowa trout fishing, you will probably confirm them on the streams. This book is for those who can appreciate the magic of small stream fishing.

If you are eager to experience excellent trout angling close to home, use this book as a guide and bear in mind that casting and fishing skills can be vitally important on small streams. If you are a spin fisherman recently converted to flyfishing, put your spin tackle in the closet for a season. After that you'll have little use for it.

1

Iowa's Trout

When I asked my son Jesse, who at the time was a relative novice to flyfishing Iowa trout streams, what he would like to see in this book, he said this: "Reassure the readers that there are actually big fish in the streams." He held his hands about 14 inches apart and said, "Not just nice fish, but," and he moved his hands to 24 inches apart, "nice *FISH!*"

And that's true. But to fully enjoy Iowa trout fishing you must also enjoy the challenge of hooking and landing fish in the 10-inch to 15-inch range in small streams that are difficult to read and a challenge to your casting technique. It is by building on that experience that you will find the larger fish that indeed are there.

Prerequisite to getting the feel of Iowa trout fishing and the streams is studying the official map published by the Department of Natural Resources. It is your source of current information on how various streams are managed and stocked, and which waters are protected by special regulations. Don't be put off by the notion that stocked fish are imbeciles that will rise to anything. As you will see, that is simply not true. Off hand I can think of only a couple of states with trout fishing, even the states renowned for it, that don't have a stocking program of one sort or another.

The state trout maps are not always available at the stores that sell fishing licenses and trout stamps. If your travels take you near the hatchery or one of the rearing stations, you can get a copy there. They are also available at the office of some of the state parks in trout country. To request one by mail, contact:

> Iowa Department of Natural Resources
> Wallace State Office Building
> Des Moines, Iowa 50319-0034
> Telephone 515-281-5145

Put-and-Take Streams

Iowa trout fishing at its best is generally brown trout fishing, and to experience it at its best you must learn to work around the Department of Natural Resources' extensive "put-and-take" program. The best way to blend your own fishing style into the program is to ignore the stocking trucks, or better still, make every attempt to avoid them. In the wake of the stocking truck come crowds of anglers whose preference is for treble hooks baited with Velveeta cheese. Avoid them, but don't cuss them. It's the fish that elude them and leave the stocking holes to take up

PUT-AND-TAKE STREAMS

Stream	Length	County	Town
Bailey's Ford	1.4	Deleware	Manchester
Bankston	2.8	Dubuque	Holy Cross
Bear	3.6	Fayette	Fayette
Bigalk	1.2	Howard	Cresco
Big Mill	4.2	Jackson	Bellevue
Bloody Run	8.5	Clayton	McGregor
Bohemian	1.2	Winneshiek	Spillville
Brush	3.8	Jackson	Maquoaeta
Buck	5.8	Clayton	Garnavillo
Clear	2.8	Allamakee	Lansing
Coldwater	1.9	Winneshiek	Burr Oak
Coon	2.2	Winneshiek	Decorah
Fountain Springs	2.4	Delaware	Greeley
French	5.0	Allamakee	Waukon
Glover's	2.0	Fayette	West Union
Grannsis	1.5	Fayette	Fayette
Ensign Hollow	2.3	Clayton	Volga
Hickory	3.3	Allamakee	Monona
Joy Spr	1.4	Deleware	Strawberry Pt
Little Mill	3.6	Jackson	Bellevue
Little Paint	1.9	Allamakee	Waterville
Little Turkey	3.0	Delaware	Colesburg
Livingood Spr.	.3	Allamakee	Postville
Maquoketa River	4.6	Delaware	Backbone Park
Mink	2.2	Fayette	Wadena
North Bear	4.2	Winneshiek	Highlandville
North Cedar	4.2	Clayton	Guttenberg
Otter	9.1	Fayette	West Union
Paint	11.2	Allamakee	Waterville
Patterson	5.8	Allamakee	Waukon
Richmond Spr	1.0	Delaware	Backbone Park
Silver	7.6	Allamakee	Waukon
Sny Magill	6.3	Clayton	Guttenberg
South Bear	4.4	Winneshiek	Highlandville
South Cedar	3.8	Clayton	Garnavillo
Spring	3.2	Mitchell	Osage
Spring Branch	1.9	Delaware	Manchester
Swiss Valley	5.6	Dubuque	Dubuque
Trout River	2.6	Winneshiek	Decorah
Trout Run	1.2	Winneshiek	Decorah
Turtle	2.7	Mitchell	St. Ansgar
Turkey River	.5	Clayton	Big Springs
Twin Springs	1.0	Winneshiek	Decorah
Village	8.3	Allamakee	Church Town
Wapsipinicon	1.8	Mitchell	McIntire
Waterloo	6.2	Allamakee	Dorchester
West Canoe	3.0	Winneshiek	Burr Oak
Wexford	1.9	Allamakee	Lansing

residence elsewhere in the stream that give fly anglers their sport fishing. I think of these as "resident" fish, but they are generally called "hold-overs" or "carry-overs."

Of the three stocked species -- brown, rainbow, and brook trout -- it is the browns that provide the best sport fishing for fly anglers. Generally rainbows are more easily caught after stocking, do not survive as well in Iowa streams as the browns, and because of a degree of steelhead blood in the strain, they have a tendency to migrate downstream, especially in the autumn. This migratory tendency has diminished somewhat with the recent introduction of the Shasta strain of rainbows, but anglers may still encounter good rainbow fishing a considerable distance below the portion of a stream that is designated as "trout waters."

Even those of us who prefer releasing most of our fish do keep a fair number of the rainbows if we want them. They make up as much as 80% of the stocking. On the other hand, brown trout are the hardiest of the group and survive well in Iowa waterways, so each individual caught should be handled carefully and released immediately. Before tying on a fly, pinch down the barb or, better still, use barbless hooks. Resident brown trout are your opportunity for a 20-inch fish someday.

Brook trout, Iowa's original native trout, do well in our streams and are lovely fish and fun to catch. They simply don't achieve the size of the browns. The stocking of brook trout (there are no natives left) was relatively limited until a pilot put-and-grow program was begun in 1992. One protected stream, South Pine, is devoted to Brook trout, so it is possible that in time we will have trophy-size brook trout.

For purposes of size comparison, disregard the state big fish records. The record holding fish are hatchery brood trout that have been moved into the streams, generally to be caught within a day or two of release. To me, using the comparatively light tackle that I do, a good day of fishing is one in which I catch several (or more) fish in the 12-inch class and one or two in the 15-inch class. In general you can apply the same size criteria to Iowa fish as those anywhere else: a 20-inch fish, particularly one caught on a #20 fly, is more than sufficient excuse to drag out the camera.

Put-and-Grow

The put-and-grow streams, sometimes called "walk-in" streams, have an immense appeal that unfortunately doesn't meet our expectations. That is not to say they don't have fish or don't have merit, but for the journeying angler they will more often than not lead to disappointment. They lend themselves well to hiking and exploring, and for the angler with ample time, some of them might indeed be productive fisheries. But when compared to the time spent actually fishing, the time spent seeking access to the streams and looking for fish in them is for most of us overwhelming. Save the put-and-grow streams for when you build your retirement cabin in the neighborhood, or allow time for exploring one at the end of your trip -- after you have had some rewarding fishing elsewhere.

When you do decide to check out these streams, spend plenty of advanced time with your maps. Rather than reproducing the alphabetical list of streams from the official map, I have rearranged the list so streams appear according to geographical proximity to one another.

Stream locations are expressed by three numbers that

appear on the trout map and on the county highway and transportation maps: Township, Range, and Section.

Township numbers appear up and down the sides of maps to indicate horizontal lines, and Range numbers indicate their vertical counterparts, with the numbers appearing across the top or bottom. At the intersection of Township and Range lines you will find the small numbered squares that are the Sections through which the stream flows.

If you have time and enjoy armchair exploring, there is great potential here, particularly if you use detailed maps. If you don't want to buy the numerous detailed topographical maps, at least use county topographicals, which you will want anyway for auxiliary help in finding the put-and-take streams.

Following are a couple of examples of how you might use the list of put-and-grow streams.

Example: You are fishing Silver Creek and wonder if there are any put-and-grow streams close by. The map shows that Silver lies roughly at T99-R5, so from the list you can see that Clear Creek at T100-R5 is the closest. When you look at the trout map you will find that indeed there is a reasonable looking route to get there. I haven't tried this example, so don't blame me...

Example: You want to devote one day to exploring put-and-grow streams, so you look for a cluster of them; how about the ones around Colesburg?

Let me add a note of caution here. *If you find a good put-and-grow stream, remember that any fish removed from it will take years to replace.* These streams are not stocked with catchable fish. You also should think twice about sharing your information with just anyone.

PUT-AND-GROW STREAMS

STREAM	COUNTY	TOWN	LOCATION
Springbrook South Fork	Jackson	Springbrook	T85-R4-S10,11,15
Big Mill	Jackson	Bellevue	T86-R4-S8,17
Hogan's Branch	Dubuque	Epworth	T88-R1-S2,3,4
Little Maquoketa	Dubuque	Epworth	T88-R1-S3,4,5
Hogan's Branch	Dubuque	Epworth	T88-R1-S2,3,4
Ram Hollow*	Delaware	Colesburg	90-R3-S11
Spring Falls	Delaware	Colesburg	90-R4-S1,2,12
Steeles Branch	Clayton	Edgewood	90-R4-S4,5,6
Grimes Hollow*	Clayton/ Deleware	Colesburg	T91-R3-S35 & T90-R3-S2,3
Pecks	Clayton	Osterdock	T91-R3-S1,11,12,14
Bear	Clayton	Edgewood	T91-R5-S23,24,25
Mossey Glen	Clayton	Strawberry Point	T91-R5-S4,9,10
Miners	Clayton	Guttenberg	T92-R2-S7,18, 20 &T92-R3-S12
Dry Mill	Clayton	Elkader	T93-R4-S8,9,16, 17,19,20
West Fork Sny-Magill	Clayton	McGregor	T94-R3-S7
Turner	Fayette	St. Lucas	T95-R9-S3,4
Teeple	Allamakee	Waukon	T97-R6-S11,14,24
Rock	Mitchell	Osage	T97-R18-S1,12 & T98-R18-S26, 35,36
Ten Mile*	Winneshiek	Decorah	T98-R9-S1,2,3
Burr Oak	Mitchell	Brownville	T98-R16-S4,5,9,10
North Canoe*	Winneshiek	Locust	T99-R8-S1,2,11,14,15
Casey Springs	Winneshiek	Decorah	T99-R9-S25,26
Pine	Winneshiek	Bluffton	T99-R9-S3,4,10 & T100-R9-S20,28, 29,33,34
Clear	Allamakee	Dorchester	T100-R5-S14,15, 22,27
Middle Bear*	Winneshiek	Highlandville	T100-R7-S14,15,16
East Pine	Winneshiek	Bluffton	T100-R9-S21,27,28
Beaver	Howard	Lime Springs	T100-R13-S21, 22,24,25,26,27,28

* Experimental brook trout stockings

2

Tackle

As the popularity of flyfishing has increased, so has the breadth of tackle, accessories, and apparel available on the market. To answer immediately the questions I am most often asked, for Iowa streams I recommend a 4-weight in a 7-foot or 7'6" rod. I change rods every couple of years in order to try out new tackle, but as of this edition I have a 6-foot 10-inch for 3-weight that I find ideal. The decision is largely determined by your casting ability, personal preferences, time available for small stream fishing, and most importantly, the number of rods you own or hope to own.

Rods

If you can dedicate a rod to small stream fishing, start by trying out a 7-foot for 4-weight and find something in that general category. If Iowa trout fishing has strong appeal to you, but the rod will also be your primary stick to use for pond fishing and such, consider an 8-foot for 5-weight.

If the small streams represent only occasional use of the rod, and it has to serve all purposes, you can't beat a 9-foot for 6-weight, which will also be your Western trout rod when you vacation in the windy mountains.

I know several fine anglers who use 9-foot rods on the Iowa streams, but the majority of serious small stream anglers use something around seven feet in length. My friend Ron, mentioned earlier, has five rods that are seven feet or shorter, each with an action that lends it to specialized use, such as nymph fishing or dry fly fishing. He even built a 5-foot rod so he can cast down the small tunnels formed by over-hanging trees on one particular stream.

If you are just starting out, here is a selection of three rods that for an Iowa angler will cover most situations:

7' for #4	Small streams worldwide
9' for #6	Lakes and ponds, especially from a canoe or float tube. Western trout, reasonable smallmouth use
9' for #8	Largemouth bass, plus pike, steelhead, and light salt water

Fly Lines

Since most small stream fishing requires relatively short casts, the difference between double taper and weight forward is negligible. Weight forward will enable you to shoot more line on casts over 30 feet, but once on the water it is impossible to mend or roll cast if the slender "running" (or "shooting") portion is on the water between you and the weight forward "head" (or "body") of the line. I generally recommend double taper for dedicated trout fishing, and weight forward for everything else, especially when the line will be used for casting practice.

Remember, it is extremely rare that you will have the full 30-foot head of a weight forward line out of the rod tip on an Iowa stream.

The lines with which I am most familiar (Cortland brand) come in a couple of varieties that differ primarily in the hardness and stiffness of the plastic coating used. The harder coated lines cast better because they slip through the guides more easily and sag less between the guides. The softer coated lines are more flexible and bend easily to drift naturally in the slow currents you often encounter on Iowa streams. I recommend the softer line for the purpose at hand. If your rod and reel are serving double duty on ponds and lakes, you might consider using a spare spool with the harder line in a bug taper for those occasions.

There is a veritable wealth of terrific fly lines these days, and a complete discussion could fill this book. Visit your pro shop and ask for advice if you are unsure. With the quality available, though, it is hard to go wrong if you stick to a brand manufactured by a reputable fly fishing company and avoid brands made by the general tackle industry.

Reels

Use a small reel that feels good to you on the rod. Backing capacity is not an issue in small streams. The presence of a disk drag is likewise of little consequence on small streams, but a good drag, which I prefer calling a "brake," in either a disc or pawl variety is essential to prevent overspooling as you strip line from the reel. Many seemingly usable garage sale reels fail drastically in this department, causing amazing "birds' nests" in your line while at the same time, for some unknown reason, attracting sand and grit like magnets.

Because of its lighter weight, I prefer the pawl (clicker) style of brake. I advise most beginners to concentrate on selecting a good rod and line first and then choosing a reel based on their budget and taste. Many anglers are either attracted to or put off by the sound of a reel. One that has an annoying sound to you in the shop will indeed wear on your nerves on a quiet stream.

Leaders and Tippets

Even more than fly line tapers and weights, leaders and tippets demand careful attention. They form the critical link to successful fly casting and fishing, and because there are many varieties on the market, I'll go into some detail here.

When you remove a new "knotless" leader from its

package, the tippet (the fine end where you attach the fly) is part of the unit. If you are using the typical 9-foot, 6X trout leader, you should carry a spool of 6X tippet material to replace tippet you lose by changing flies. The "X" designation represents thousandths of an inch in diameter, with 0X equaling .011, 1X equaling .010, and so forth.

Standard procedure is to carry an assortment of tippet material so leaders can be customized to changing fishing conditions. For example, when fishing smooth, slow water you need fine tippet, usually 6X or even 7X, that will allow your flies to drift naturally on the surface. (We call it "drag" when the leader prevents your fly from drifting naturally.) Envision the trout in the stream, facing into the current, watching the panorama passing over its head. It is essential that your fly drifts just like the cottonwood seed and piece of bark that are floating along with it.

Using small flies, #18 and down, and fine tippet is typical in slow water. In faster, rippled water it is typical to go to larger flies that are more visible to both you and the fish. That calls for a heavier tippet so the cast unrolls to the full length of the leader. The same is true when the wind comes up. Many of us are guilty of not changing tippet size as we make changes in fly size, and it costs us fish.

In addition to the size of tippet material, be aware that individual brands vary in stiffness and ability to turn over a fly at the end of the cast. When selecting tippet material and leaders, notice that for any given size, the breaking weights are different for different brands of material. Those with the higher test strength are softer and will flow better in a slow current and stretch more before breaking, but they will not turn the fly over as well as their lower test, stiffer counterparts.

For nymph fishing you might consider a 7' 6" leader

and add to it another foot or so of tippet; the resulting knot will keep your split shot from sliding down to the fly.

Common practice is to install a "permanent leader butt" on the fly line so leaders can be replaced without cutting away any of the fly line's tip. A permanent leader butt consists of three or four inches of heavy monofilament that ends in a tiny loop (preferably a Perfection Loop) which in turn mates with a loop tied at the end of the leader's butt section. If the permanent butt is fashioned from brightly colored monofilament it doubles as a strike indicator to watch when fishing nymphs.

Many anglers have found that tying their own complete leaders from varying sizes of monofilament increases their ability to turn over the fly. Hand tied leaders are also available commercially.

Nets

Although many anglers fish without one, I recommend using a "catch-and-release" style of net. I believe that it is easier on the fish to play him less and land him in a net rather than having to squeeze him in your hand to bring him under control. Catch-and-release netting is available for nets in the traditional shape.

Gadgets and Accessories

Along with the rod, reel, line, and leader you need fly floatant, a split shot assortment and strike indicators, nippers to cut and trim the leader, and a hemostat or other type of hook remover that you can also use to pinch down the barb of your hooks.

Additional useful items will usually work their way onto your "necessities" list. They include the Ty-Rite tools, which I personally rely on heavily, along with various lights and magnifying accessories and fly drying devices. Leaders are best straightened by hand rather than pulling them through a "straightener." A firm, steady pull does the trick.

As you become more and more familiar with the insect life of the streams, a small seine is valuable. Some anglers also carry a thermometer.

To keep yourself honest, a piece of tape at a measured distance on your rod is superior to carrying a measuring tape. If you carry a scale to weigh the true trophy fish, adjust it to read zero with your net attached so you can weigh the fish in the net without additional handling.

Waders and Apparel

My very strong opinion is that 3- or 4-millimeter neoprene chest waders will contribute to your success nearly as much as a good rod, maybe more. The felt sole on the boots, whether they are separate wading shoes or shoes built onto the waders, will give you sure footing. The height will allow you to negotiate passage through deeper water to get around logs and rocks, and it will also allow you to kneel in the stream to place a strategic cast.

In general, you will cause much less commotion if you can simply stay in the stream. During very hot days in shallow water, neoprene chest waders can be rolled down to waist level; during the coldest of winter days you can stay warm with additional layers of clothing underneath.

For streams that you know to be shallow, neoprene hippers are good auxiliary wading gear.

Most anglers wear a vest, the invention of the late master angler Lee Wulff. Increasing the number of pockets raises the cost of the vest, while at the same time causing the possibility of confusion and the certainty of carrying too much stuff. My advice is to go easy on the pockets and the dollars, but do make sure that your vest has the large cargo pocket on the back to carry your rain jacket, lunch, and water supply.

There are times when a day pack is very useful for carrying your waders so you can change into them after a long hike.

For headwear, the baseball cap is most popular, but I like the extra protection of a Western style hat or a long billed cap. By all means, wear something, even a visor, to reduce glare off the water and keep miscreant flies away from your eyes and face. In most situations you should also wear polarized sun glasses, which help immensely in locating fish.

For clothing, there is currently a trend toward wearing camouflage. If you're comfortable in camo, it probably helps a little. If you're self-conscious in it, at least think about wearing something with a broken pattern. The whole issue strikes me as deserving a place far down the list of important concerns, but sometimes details can make or break you. In some situations you are very visible to the fish.

Lastly I want to mention rain jackets of the type called steelhead jackets. A couple of years ago I received one that cost more than I would ever have considered spending for any jacket. But today, if something were to happen to it, I would replace it immediately without batting an eye. It has paid me tenfold its cost in days that I've fished in comfort that before I would not have fished at all.

3

Basic Fly Selection

There are frequent suggestions for fly patterns throughout the text, but for beginners, the following page contains a list of flies with which you should be able to catch fish almost anytime, anywhere in Iowa (or the world, for that matter). Following the list are a few comments on colors and seasonal use of the flies. If you are a newcomer to the ranks of flyfishing, note that the category I show as simply "Dry Flies" would, in a longer list, be further divided into three categories -- attractors (Humpy), imitators (Elkhair Caddis), and terrestrials (hoppers).

Basic Iowa Trout Flies

Type	Name	Size
Nymphs	Pheasant Tail	12 - 20
	Gold Ribbed Hare's Ear	"
	Prince	"
Dry Flies	Elk Hair Caddis	14 - 18
	(assorted colors)	
	Royal Wulff or Humpy	12 - 20
	Coachman Trude or	
	Goddard Caddis	12 - 14
	Mosquito	18 - 20
	Hoppers	4 - 8
	Griffith Gnat	
	or Renegade	18 - 20
Wet Flies	Soft Hackles	14 - 18
	Scuds	14 - 16
	Leadwing Coachman	12 - 14
	Serendipity	18 - 20

Here are some good flies to add to the list above:

Type	Name	Size
Nymphs	Zug Bug	14 - 18
	Brassie	"
	Muskrat Nymph	12 - 16
Dry Flies	Ants	16 - 18
	Adams	14 - 20
	Various spinners	14 - 20
	Various Mayfly imitations	12 - 20
Others	Woolly Worms	4 - 14
	Streamers	2 - 6

The last two entries on the Dry Fly list opposite are deliberately vague. The only scholarly work I've seen on Iowa trout stream insects concludes that because of marginal water quality, caddisflies are much more prevalent than Mayflies. Some Mayfly patterns to try along with the Adams are Light and Dark Hendricksons, Pale Morning Duns, Comparaduns, and Blue-wing Olives.

The important thing to remember is that when you encounter an insect hatch of any sort, match the size first and then the color. Identifying the insects will come later, or it won't, depending on the extent of your interest. It is not essential to catching fish. I've used a Colorado guide who dipped his seine in the water to gather a sample that he held up and scrutinized carefully before proclaiming, "Well, it's about yea big and cream colored."

In his fly box we found something about the right size and color and he tied it on my leader. Within seconds I hooked a trophy fish.

The easiest way to start learning insects is by fishing with someone who can teach you. The least you should learn is to distinguish caddisflies from Mayflies. The flies included in the first list above are ones I consider essential, and I carry at least two or three of each size at all times.

In the spring, black caddisfly patterns are very productive. Later on, tan or light brown work well.

It should go without saying, but you should fish with hopper patterns through the summer months and into early autumn, as long as you see the real thing in the grass.

The soft hackles and the Serendipity, like the other wet flies, are fished in the film where they resemble emerging insects that trout intercept just below the surface. It is sometimes hard to tell whether the fish you see rising are taking insects off the surface or from just below the surface. Before you go crazy trying to match a hatch, try tying on an emerger pattern first.

Most anglers follow the time honored practice of using darker flies in off-color water and on dark days. Doing so at least gives you a starting point in fly selection. In high, fast water after a rain, try using scuds or other large wet flies.

Yogi Berra is quoted as saying, "You observe a lot by just watching." That pretty well sums up the best approach to learning trout streams and their insects. The more time you spend on the water, the more details you will come to see. It is a skill some of us try to develop consciously to offset the years we've spent outdoors trying to repel, kill, or at least ignore the insects around us.

4

Fishing Small Streams

The first season I fly fished, as a ten-year-old with a long cane rod, I began each morning by working the entire shoreline of our large farm pond, starting and finishing the circuit always at the same willow tree. One morning by chance I reached the water a little early and saw departing from my customary starting place a large, let's say huge, dorsal fin. The fish had been lying just a couple of feet from shore at the exact spot where I normally planted my feet to start casting. The following morning, nearly trembling, I stopped 20 feet shy of the water, and by false casting off to the side, coaxed out enough line to drop my McGinty right at the water's edge where I'd seen the fin. Wham! Flashing orange in morning sun, up came one of, if not the, largest bluegills caught in the 35 years we owned and managed the pond.

Today I am careful to be certain my clients understand that when I point out a likely spot, it is their fly, not their feet, that I want them to put there. My personal feeling is that most of us are harboring instincts, or at least accumulations of experiences, that will lead us to fish if we follow them with less enthusiasm and more wisdom. Rather than concentrating on stealth, I prefer simply fishing in tempo and in harmony with the waters. Slower, gentler sections where you see occasional diligent rises must be fished with a soft, deliberate touch, while faster, rougher waters can be worked more aggressively.

Only occasionally do I approach the water on my hands and knees.

All of this is said simply to emphasize the fact that by nature trout are extremely wary while humans are very clumsy.

Upstream and Down

Trout generally face into the current, which means you should fish upstream. If that isn't possible, for example if you park at a bridge with a partner and you want to go in opposite directions, you should walk well away from the stream as you proceed down. Your choice then is to either walk downstream the entire distance you plan to fish, or to fish individual spots that you see as you proceed down, approaching each in turn from downstream.

As you proceed along a stream, you are looking for either rising fish or good holding water. When fishing upstream you can begin with a nymph and replace it with an emerger or dry fly when you encounter rising fish. When walking downstream, I pass by holding water, memorizing its location, and am tempted to stop and work a run or pool only if there is a promising rise. Even then I may memorize it for later and move on down the entire distance I plan to fish. On new water this gives you the chance to survey it before fishing it.

When you wade upstream in strange waters, even wearing polarized glasses won't insure that you don't waste time on water that when viewed from a different angle, like the bank above, is obviously too slow and shallow to hold fish under normal circumstances. That same water might be teeming with fish in the evening when there is a hatch, but during warm days the fish will be in deeper pools and runs nearby. Some Iowa streams have as few as two or three good pools in the course of a mile, and a novice can spend an entire day carefully fishing barren water.

If a stream is unfamiliar to you, take a hike and assess the waters before you start fishing in earnest, making sure that you and your shadow stay a respectable distance from the water.

Likewise, and I think this is important, when you first find a stream from your car, drive a ways in both directions and explore it from your auto before deciding where to begin. My unfortunate first Iowa trout excursion was memorable in that it was the first time ever that I fished too much and drove too little. To this day I devote a portion of each trip to exploring new streams both on foot and on wheels.

The object of all this walking and exploring is to find holding water, the water where the fish live (as opposed to the water where, for example, they go out to dinner). Trout need relatively cool, highly oxygenated water. Cold water holds oxygen better than warm, but trout can tolerate higher water temperatures if there is sufficient oxygen present. A bubbling riffle six inches deep might hold fish while a slow moving run of much greater depth might not.

Following is a synopsis of the various types of holding water.

Pools

Pools are deep water with a relatively calm surface, with either a run or a riffle at each end. The upstream end is called the head and the downstream end the tail. If there is a riffle coming into the pool you know that because of the turbulence in the riffle the water there will be high in oxygen. Be careful not to overlook pools because of their size. I can think of several on Spring Branch Creek that are barely large enough to submerge a kitchen chair, yet they hold numerous large browns.

Runs

Runs are long, narrow stretches much like pools, but with swifter current (but still a relatively flat surface). If deep enough to remain cool they hold fish well. Because of the current they often have undercut banks, which are the classic hiding place for the big ones. There are often weeds hanging out over the water making runs ideal places to drop in a hopper pattern.

If either a pool or a run is situated on a bend or curve in the stream, look for the deepest water to be on the outside of the curve. There is an adage used by rivermen that holds true more often than not: "The steep side's the deep side." The side that has the higher bank is likely to have the deeper water.

Holes

More common in vernacular than print is the term "hole." Holes are diminutive pools, sometimes unpredictably situated. Ones that I find fish in often occur where the creek bends sharply around a tree, gouging a deep hole and exposing lots of roots. Like some pools that are unapproachable from below, you might have to fish this type of hole from upstream, using a weighted nymph and feeding line out quickly as the current takes it down across the hole.

Not all holes have the tree roots. Some may be above or below a rock in midstream, others may be near a downfall, and others may just be there.

Holding water may make up one-half or more of a stream or be limited to only a few pools. The remaining water is usually riffles and shallow runs.

Riffles

Riffles, the little rapids that make up a sizable length of most streams, are high in oxygen but cause the fish to work harder while he's in them. You generally find fish there in the evenings when they come into the riffles because of a heavy hatch.

Working the Water

To work any piece of water effectively, begin fishing close to you and work progressively farther out. In still pools, false cast to rid your line of water, even if your fly doesn't need drying, and be sure the false casts are directed so the line and its shadow don't fall over fish (or likely spots for fish). It sounds extreme, but many anglers can benefit from spending some time at the kitchen table drawing pictures of differently shaped pools and adding lines to indicate where they would place the first, second, third cast, and so forth.

There are as many different styles as there are anglers. Some anglers fish nymphs almost exclusively and use less that a foot of line outside the rod tip, flipping the fly forward just the length of the leader. Others may stay back from the stream to cast a fairly long length of line. Still others roll cast frequently.

If you have approached fish quietly from behind and see them close in front of you, let the drift continue completely over them, nearly to you or, especially with a nymph, even on past you. If at the end of the drift the leader and a little line are still in front of you, a roll cast pickup is in order. If the line has passed beyond you downstream, wait until it has straightened out its full length, with the rod tip lowered, then simply cast it back upstream as though you were picking up a normal backcast.

Regardless of your personal approach, fish carefully and make as little disturbance as possible. Bear in mind that familiarity with a stream doesn't stop with learning where the fish are, but carries into knowing the best way to work each bit of the water. Even in streams only three or four feet wide, the current in the center will be so swift that for your fly to drift along the edge without dragging you must cast from the side you want to fish, not across the current.

Take your time. Fish with your rod tip down and your line hand ready. In many students I see that line handling problems are more of an obstacle to successful angling than casting problems. Awkward line handling also causes as many snarls and tangles as poor casting does.

In some situations the stream might appear barren, and in your eagerness to find the next pool you can overlook many good holes. On other streams there is such good water and there are so many fish that you must scrutinize the stream literally foot by foot to keep from overlooking the largest fish in the least obvious places.

My approach is to cover carefully any water that looks promising while wasting as little time as possible on marginal water. Don't get so absorbed in studying the water that you forget to look for fish. In a decent stream you should see some on a normal day. To learn to see fish more easily, try looking for their shadows first.

5

Changing Conditions

I'm regularly regaled with tales of woe from anglers who have had a poor trip to the Iowa streams, and more often than not it's because they were not ready for the fishing conditions they encountered. Indeed, anticipating conditions is a skill that can never be totally mastered. From the relatively protected location of my shop, it's easy for me to forget that Saylorville Lake, just fifteen minutes away, is under a small craft advisory. During the three hours it takes me to drive to Manchester, the weather can change drastically and, as important as it might be, weather is just one of the variables that effect success.

In the process of getting ready for a trip, we construct elaborate imaginary scenes, all of which include ourselves ultimately catching fish. Having more experience doesn't necessarily mean that we build more accurate images; it means we build more of them: Us catching fish in the wind, us catching fish in the rain, us catching fish in crowds of other anglers, and so forth.

Even then, for a typical Iowa outing, there are so many variables that alone, or even with the help of several partners, you won't have imagined them all. You might not readily imagine the herd of Holstein cows, for example. Or you might arrive at Bloody Run to find that Clayton is the only Iowa county that's had rain in two weeks, and it fell last night.

Here, then, is some advice on dealing with common situations.

Fishing Pressure

The easiest way to avoid crowded conditions is the obvious one -- fish during the week. If you are restricted by a rigid work situation, consider using a vacation day or two each season. You may not have the stream entirely to yourself, but the pressure should at least be reasonable. Here, in no particular order, are a few recommended times and methods to beat the weekend pressure. The extreme hours I suggest are also some of the best hours for fishing.

Sunday mornings. For reasons ranging from attending church to nursing hangovers, much of humankind isn't available for the trout stream on Sunday mornings. You can be the exception.

Mornings at dawn. Use a light to get to the stream, but don't shine it on the water. You are likely to have the water entirely to yourself, and it's an excellent time to fish. Try putting a big streamer in front of a big brown that you've had your eye on.

The last hour of daylight. This is my favorite time to fish, and it never fails to surprise me that most folks head for their homes or campfires before it is actually dark. Dusk is also good dry fly time, often with predictable evening hatches. (By that I mean you can predict that there will be an evening hatch and the accompanying dry fly action, not that you can predict what the hatch will be.)

During the long days of summer, fishing with the earliest morning light and latest evening light gives you a good excuse for a nap or a trip to town during the heat of the afternoon when the fishing tends to be off anyway. Carry a light to find your way back to your car in the evening.

Take a hike. That's all there is to it. Most people, even typically industrious ones, don't walk very far to fish. It's amazing how many people you can leave behind with a short hike.

Avoid stocking days. Most local bait anglers keep tabs on the stocking trucks, so the more days that have passed since it was last seen, the fewer other anglers there'll be. Likewise, don't hesitate to try the streams that the DNR quits stocking in hot weather. The fact that they don't stock them doesn't mean the fish are all gone or dead.

Winter. I could also say early spring and late autumn, but "winter" covers it all. One day last January, after three consecutive days of -20 degrees, the forecasters rightly predicted +20. John Pursell and I were there to catch rising rainbows using a #20 Renegade, Griffith Gnat, or Serendipity, while another angler on the stream was doing well with Gold Ribbed Hare's Ear nymphs.

Autumn! I know this is redundant with the paragraph above, but it astounds me how drastically fishing activity drops off when school starts and televised football leaps from hibernation. My harsh opinion is that if you bypass this best, loveliest season, you forfeit the right to complain about summer crowds.

Fish isolated streams. Once you have tried some of the streams discussed in Part II, seek out and try others. On my most recent trip, everybody from an innkeeper to a store clerk to a conservation officer told me different hot spots, especially after I let it be known that I flyfished. Offhand, I'd say that two out of three or more of the tips contained at least some sound advice.

Wait your turn. I don't mean that you should sit and glare at someone already fishing a pool, but neither should you think that someone else's having been there first has ruined it. Fish recover quickly if a pool, even a calm one, is "rested" for a few minutes. Who knows? Your presentation and fly selection could be just what the fish have been waiting for. In faster water with a rippled surface, an almost continuous parade of anglers can pass without spooking the fish. Use weighted nymphs, hair-wing attractors, or Goddard Caddis patterns in this situation.

Etiquette

No matter what you do, whether in Iowa or elsewhere, there will be times when someone will intrude rudely on your fishing. Often it will be a spinfisher who doesn't realize how much room fly casting takes or how much area a fly angler can cover from one position. Amongst fly anglers, etiquette is largely a matter of common sense, usually based on the newcomer following the first angler upstream. If the first angler is working slowly, you can jump in ahead of him or her by leaving a substantial distance of stream -- a couple of good pools, for example -- between you. Just put yourself in his shoes.

The more anglers on a stream, the less space gets left between them. On the most crowded waters, minimum space between anglers should still leave generous room for casting and playing fish. In this resepect, Spring Branch Creek is similar to the Yellowstone River -- the next angler might be just 50 feet away, but there are probably scores of fish between the two of you. The only time you fish that closely to someone else is when there is no other room. You certainly never "cut in line" to get to a choice pool.

If it seems appropriate, don't hesitate to clear your intentions with the angler already there. You will find that if you simply ask, for example, "Do you mind if I start ahead of you up at the bridge?" the answer will often be, "Start at the next pool up if you want. I've got to leave after I'm done here."

The determining factor is giving the fish you have disturbed a chance to recover before the next fisher gets there.

Private Land

Many streams run through private land.
Some begin on state-owned land and continue on through
private land. We all know enough not to litter, but even
more important to farmers is the preservation of their fences.
The stiles, seemingly invitations to fish in the stream, are actually there to protect the fence. Please, don't change fishing conditions by causing a landowner to close a section of
stream because you damaged his fences.

Weather and Water

Trout, already wet and cold and perpetually
wary of attack from above, prefer different weather than we
do. At least that's a useful way to think about it. The fish
themselves probably don't have strong preferences about
weather, as such, but rather the protection from view
provided by some cloud cover, a little drizzle, or a breeze to
ruffle the water's surface. Also entering the equation is the
availability of food. The more food there is around, the
more daring the fish will be, regardless of visibility. Their
survival depends on eating as much as possible while ex-
pending the least amount of energy.

When conditions are borderline, a small change can
be significant. On French Creek during my last visit, the
fish at midday would rise each time one of the thin, puffy
clouds darkened the sky just a fraction, but not when the sun
was shining full strength.

Weather and water conditions could be the subject of a
long dissertation, but I doubt that it would be of much value,

especially when compared to experience. Essentially there are two things under your control that, along with versatile clothing, will enhance your chances through the changes of weather -- fly selection and casting skill.

Fly Selection

Here is where the imaginary scenes I mentioned at the beginning of this chapter can really work against you. The first mental picture you will have of a stream is the one left over from the last time you fished there. If the water then was flat and the fish were rising to Elk Hair Caddis, that is what you will anticipate as you sit at the tying bench or make purchases at the fly shop.

I typically have a couple of hundred flies with me, often more, and at times I still get caught without the pattern I need because of a simple oversight. During my last visit to Emsign Hollow I would gladly have traded half of the five or six dozen Humpies and Wulffs I had for just one tinsel-ribbed streamer or muddler minnow. The stream was off color and it turned out to be one of the rare occasions when a spin fisherman with Panther Martins outfished me. I know streamers would have worked if only I'd had some.

Other flies to use in high or colored water are Woolly Buggers, San Juan Worms, and Scuds (the latter only if there is watercress in the stream). When the surface of a pool is rough, or the fish are out in riffles and choppy runs, larger attractors can work as well as nymphs. Be aware that the way the wing is tied on Coachman Trudes (we call it a "down" wing) gives them a caddisfly profile that is often better in Iowa waters than the upright wing on Wulffs and other hairwing attractors.

High water doesn't necessarily mean colored water. When it's high and clear, a classic wet fly like a Leadwing Coachman is worth a try.

As you expand your fly selection, don't neglect adding a few spinners (the patterns tied with the wings sticking straight out the sides).

The usual solution to getting a strike from reluctant fish is to go smaller. If there is a hatch going on and you can't get a hit, try a soft hackle fly in case the fish are taking emergers, and if that fails, try showing them something big and ugly and out of place, like a Woolly Bugger. The technique of "changing the rules," for example using a big fly during a midge hatch, is often productive when you're otherwise stumped.

Casting

Among the common complaints that unsuccessful anglers register with me are wind, high grass and standing weeds along streams, aquatic vegetation in the streams, spooky fish on bright days, and pools that are unaccessible because of overhanging tree branches. Most of these problems diminish not only as your casting skills develop, but also as you get better at approaching the stream. Many casting problems are really problems with your position.

A savvy angler will walk unbelievable distances to approach a worthwhile fish from the best spot. If you study the situation long enough you can usually find a position from which to cast. Sometimes you will select a position and see a better one once you have gotten there. In regard to all of this, the worst mistake you can make is trying to fish without waders. Some streams can be managed in only hip boots, but it's only in retrospect that you'll know that. As mentioned earlier, neoprene chest waders enhance your ability to catch fish.

There are some anglers who will argue, but casting in my opinion is as important as choice of flies. There is no such think as the "wrong" fly if it's properly presented, whereas a poor presentation with the "right" fly will spook not just one, but many fish.

There are two stages of development in casting. The first is developing the ability to cast effectively under practice conditions; the second is applying that ability on a trout stream. In the practice phase, there are three common faults I see, two of which are related and occur during the back cast. For a good back cast, you must stop the rod tip quickly and high in its path. For beginners this is typically overhead around one o'clock. At that point it is essential to wait for the line to straighten out behind you before beginning the forward cast. Not stopping the rod properly, and not letting the line straighten out, are common but easily repaired faults.

The third common problem is knowing where to stop the power in the forward cast, which I express in term of "aiming." If the forward cast is aimed too high the line will fall to the water in a heap. If aimed too low it will unroll across the water, if it straightens out at all, making a tremendous commotion. The cast should straighten out in the air and fall gently to the water, fully straightened out.

On the trout stream, accuracy in tight quarters and the

ability to straighten out not only the line, but at least a 9-foot leader, are absolute necessities. Accuracy is enhanced by the ability to cast tight loops, which also are your defense against the wind. A tight loop will simply fit into more places and travel better through the wind. False casting is the practice technique I recommend for working on loops, and if you want professional help, casting workshops are available throughout the country. So important is casting that professional guides are expected to coach anglers in casting techniques in addition to finding fish.

To straighten out the full length of leader so it lands delicately without spooking fish in slow, calm water, the line must be traveling fast. Among anglers who cast well and form nice loops in practice yet struggle on the streams, the most frequent problem I see is the ability to develop line speed.

The common solution is a technique called "hauling." A haul is simply a short quick tug of the line away from the rod with the line hand. You can do it as you pick line up from the water, and again as you release it on the forward cast. The quick haul on the forward cast will add all the speed necessary to straighten out the leader and give you more efficiency in the wind.

If you have good control over the basic techniques described above, experiment with hauling. ("Double hauling" is a little more complicated and is used to gain distance, rarely a concern on Iowa streams.)

With practice and experience, wind and brush can be conquered by good casting. Aquatic growth requires accuracy to hit the open spots, but often prohibits the use of nymphs. Dry flies and wet flies like soft hackles fished in the film can be drifted over watercress. Expect strikes as your fly drifts over openings in the vegetation.

When casting weighted nymphs or casting with split shot on the line, delicacy of presentation is not a factor. Anglers who fish nymphs regularly develop a snappy casting style based on short, quick strokes that speed the line quickly (and safely) past them in the air.

Changing Streams

There is very little I can recommend that will help you prepare for changes in the streams themselves. You simply have to be mentally prepared. If your last visit to a pool was in the spring, be ready for grass and weeds up to your shoulders in late summer. Last year's nicely cut alfalfa field could be head-high corn this season. Wet or dry seasons will create and destroy pools. Beaver dams appear in places you would never expect. Huge logs in the stream wash away, or trees topple into the stream.

If there is a new suggestion to add here, it is that you take your bearings from permanent, or at least enduring, landmarks. Don't think of a particular riffle as being next to the cornfield. Instead, look for a rock formation to help you return to the spot. This is true also in merely finding the stream. Fields and even buildings can be fickle landmarks.

The approach I use to learn a new stream is to find every parking area and fence crossing, getting out of the car and walking a ways upstream and downstream. I also stop and get out at all bridges to watch the water for awhile.

Once you get your bearings and have fished the "easy"

spots, let intuition be your guide -- is this section worth a day's effort to walk the required miles of water? The most successful anglers I know are the ones whose instincts say "yes." And with most of us, our feet all too often say "no."

Part II

The Streams

6

Iowa Trout Streams

The streams discussed in this section have been included for one or more reasons. First, of course, are the well-known streams I consider best for flyfishing. They are ones that have a demonstrated ability to sustain good fish populations under the current regulations. Along with them are streams that I have included because of their location. In general, the streams seem to improve the farther north you travel, but for the purpose at hand I wanted to include streams from all parts of the trout country.

A few streams have found their way into these pages because of their proximity to other, better streams. Those streams, Joy Springs is an example, still have some redeeming features that warrant their inclusion. There are times in our sporting lives, or I feel there should be, when the quality of the stream is secondary to the quality of the picnic area or playgrounds, when the colorful villages with antique shops and riverboats add measurably to our enjoyment of trout country.

And there is the matter of campgrounds too. Just like you can wet a line at Joy Springs while stopping for a picnic lunch, likewise you can take your rod for an evening stroll along Twin Springs while the coals under the grill burn down. You can do that at lower Bloody Run too, and then visit the riverboat casino after supper.

Maps and Signs

The official trout map distributed by the Iowa Department of Natural Resources is, as I mentioned earlier, indispensable. It is based on the Iowa Department of Transportation's county transportation maps, and for that reason does not show the streams themselves as well as the U.S. Geological Survey's topographical maps. Those, of course, show both streams and roads in great detail, but they include very few road names or numbers.

The maps I have included here were produced by transcribing the roads and streams from the topographical maps and adding road designations from the transportation maps and, more importantly, from personal experience.

This is important: If you try to navigate the back roads with the trout map or other published maps, you will find that often the county road numbers are not posted as you would expect to find them, sometimes not at all.

Part of the problem stems from the fact that to initiate the Emergency 911 telephone system, every street in a township had to be assigned a name or number. Thus you find 340th Avenue about as far from a town as you can get in Iowa. For some reason there are now county roads that are marked with street names on traditional street signs, while the pentagon-shaped county road signs have disappeared. For example, at this time Clayton county road W67 is marked only with street signs indicating "St. Sebald Road." There are no W67 signs. This might change, but what won't change is the sporadic nature of road signs.

This holds true also for the nice little signs, brown with yellow lettering, that in many places indicate trout streams. For every place that has one there is another place that should have one and does not. For reasons I'll leave you to ponder, they simply get torn down. Some very popular streams like Sny Magill currently have none at all. You can often get a clue to stream location from either the small green and white Game Management Area signs, or, on the main roads, the brown and white Conservation Commission signs that point toward public areas.

Because the maps here are large in scale, the curves in the road do not appear to be as sharp as they are in reality. The twists and bends in the stream, however, are more easily followed and are, for the most part, quite accurate.

Finding Your Way

Since my earliest days of driving Iowa's back roads I have used an auto compass. The times I've used a car or truck without one, I've missed it or even regretted it. I've lived in remote areas and keep my bearings pretty well, but before and after daylight hours, or even on a cloudy day, it is all too easy to lose track of direction on winding roads, especially if you are looking for help from signs that don't exist.

Keep your gas tank filled. The last wrong turn I took

was before dawn when I left my planned route because of a gasoline crisis I could have easily avoided. On another occasion I ran completely dry right at dark. Some towns don't have a gas pump, and some that do might keep shorter hours than you think they should. Be sure to fill on Saturday night in case the stations along your route on Sunday morning are closed.

On foot there is the chance of getting lost if you don't retrace your exact route. Here is a common mistake to avoid: Instead of following the stream back to your starting point, you decide to cut across a hill that the stream has curved around, and in the process you intersect and follow a different stream. Hunters encounter this problem by heading down the wrong ravine from a hilltop and find themselves at the base of the hill on a road miles from their car. Even in Iowa it doesn't hurt to watch your back trail and keep count of the number of streams you cross.

There are two ways to approach fishing many of these streams, you can drive around in your car and fish the obvious holes close to the road, or you can set out and fish the entire length of the water. Both methods have merit. When you elect to fish the entire length of a stream, consider taking a day pack with a rain jacket, a light lunch, and importantly, water. Most of us neglect drinking enough water, especially when hiking.

Among the more rugged treks on Iowa's streams are the protected area of Bloody Run and the lower section of French Creek. Those places and others could be approached sensibly with two vehicles, as you would a float trip.

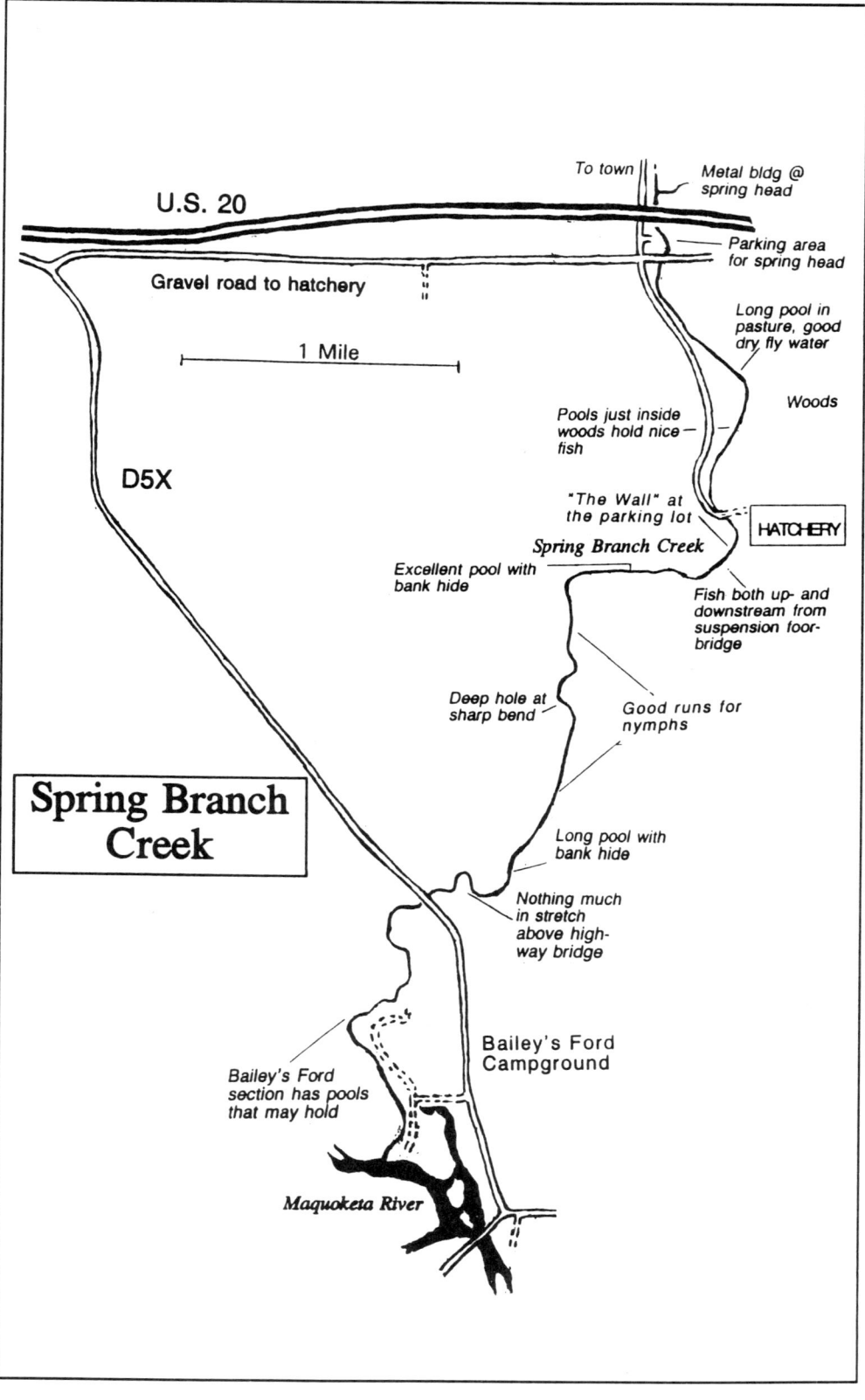

7

Spring Branch Creek

Spring Branch Creek is most often referred to with a single adjective -- tough. That makes it seem contradictory that it is also the stream that I most often recommend to beginning trout anglers.

Frequently referred to simply as "Manchester," this special-regulation spring creek runs for 2.9 miles, from the spring head just north of Iowa Route 20, through the grounds of the trout hatchery, under county road D5X, and into the Maquoketa River at Bailey's Ford country park. On the trout map the last mile is referred to as Bailey's Ford, and that stretch of water is not protected.

After the word "tough," every angler should think four additional words: Hawkeye Fly Fishing Association. It is through the HFFA members' sustained initiative that this stream is the fishery that it is. Club members have effected all of the bank improvements, kept the stream clean, and influenced its designation as a protected stream. Only artificial lures are allowed, and there is a length limit on all trout.

Although it's tough to hook and land large fish, which are plentiful, there is no problem in locating fish. It is a rare day indeed that you can't find rising fish somewhere in the creek, even in the dead of winter. And while the resident fish are what I call "PH.D fish," there are usually enough recent escapees from the hatchery and other remedial level fish that a beginner can usually be successful.

More experienced anglers can hone their total fishing skill to a keen edge. Many of us have experienced immediate success on notorious rivers like Idaho's Henry's Fork because of disciplines learned on Spring Branch Creek.

So important do I consider this stream that I have drawn a "treasure map" to facilitate your first visits. After a few visits I encourage you to explore harder, looking for trophy fish where you least expect them. It is the epitome of the old saying about not being able to see the forest for the trees. Here there are, at times at least, so many fish in sight that you have trouble focusing on the best ones.

Here is an example of how you should learn to look at the stream: Fly tackle rep and former Yellowstone guide Kurt Weieneth and I were discussing, in great detail, a section of the creek no more than 15 yards long. After some talking I produced the inevitable scrap of paper and Kurt drew a detailed map showing exactly which grass-covered clump of dirt next to the bank hide was sheltering the 19" brown he had failed to induce to strike. (It was Kurt's first trip to the stream; he was certain that a size 24 or 26 dry of almost any sort would have gotten some action.)

All of the flies recommended in Chapter 3 are good here. There are brook trout along with the browns and rainbows, particularly near the spring head where you find water cress and consequently scuds. Scuds, San Juan Worms, and classic wet flies are particularly effective when the water is high and the fish are out feeding in the riffles. A rain storm will bring the creek's level up dramatically, but such little land area is drained by the water shed the level can return to normal in just a few hours.

During the summer months, Spring Branch is an excellent stream for hopper patterns. In the winter, Renegades or Griffith Gnats make convincing snow midge imitations.

Finding Spring Branch

Approaching on Route 20 from the west, take the second Manchester exit (the first if you are coming from the east). Either ramp will stop you facing west, so proceed to the left, away from town and toward Bailey's Ford, for just less than a mile. Take the first gravel road turning left. Your first and only stop will be at the surfaced road leading to the hatchery. At that point there will be visible to your left a parking area near the spring house. Turn right to reach the hatchery where the stream skirts the parking lot. I recommend allowing time to visit the hatchery before you begin fishing because, if you're like most of us, you'll get hung up on a fish that will keep you busy until dark.

Spring Branch Creek makes an ideal one-night outing. Camping at Bailey's Ford is convenient, and Manchester is a pleasant town with several motels and a variety of eateries. To reach town from the hatchery you don't need to retrace your route on the gravel; just take the hardtop out of the hatchery and follow it under the four lane until you reach the highway, then turn left to go about two miles into town.

Fishing pressure can be considered heavy at times, if

that sort of thing bothers you. I generally fish there during the week by leaving Des Moines midmorning, fishing the evening hatches, and fishing again early the following morning before starting home. The adventure takes little more that 24 hours and it feels like two days of fishing. (See earlier notes on fishing pressure.)

If you do fish this stream when it feels crowded to you, be patient and courteous and you will get a turn at every pool. Most anglers depart before that prime final hour of light. Carry a flashlight and fish until it is absolutely too dark to continue.

8

Other Protected Streams

As you will notice when reading the descriptions of the various streams, different sections of different streams have been protected at one time or another. By the time you read this book there may again have been changes affecting which areas are either protected or not protected by special regulations.

Ensign Hollow

Ensign Hollow, the recipient in the early 1990's of extensive HFFA work of the same sort performed at Spring Branch Creek, receives mixed reviews from visiting anglers. In character, Ensign is like two totally different streams stuck together end-to-end, so before you can take anybody's word about the stream you have to know which part of it they fished.

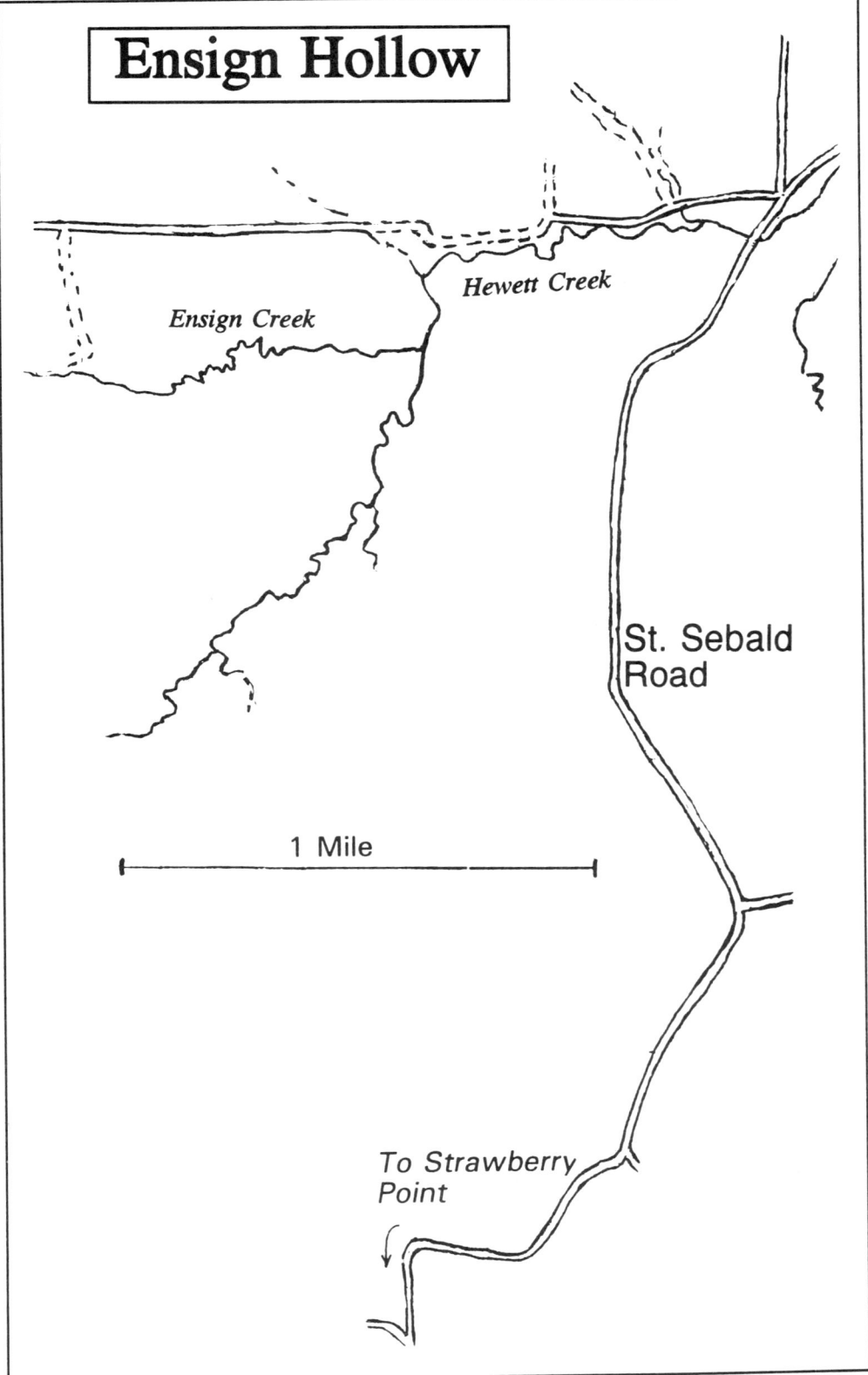

When you locate the stream and follow the lane upstream to the small parking area, roughly in the middle of its length, you pass the lower end that is private pasture through which the stream winds in a series of pools, runs and riffles. Except for a few thistles, it is like a golf course, only better because of the trout.

From the parking area upstream the land is owned by the state and thus is not mowed. This is also the section of the stream to which the improvements have been made, and the result is that you have a virtually endless bank hide that winds its way tediously through a jungle of tall grass. This frustrates many anglers. It is tricky indeed to keep your casts out of the weeds and in the water, but personally, I find this schizophrenic little stream to be fun.

The bottom section holds more fish than you might expect. As usual, keep a lookout for rising fish, and drift a Goddard Caddis or your favorite nymph around some of the deep bends. The upper portion, with all the growth hanging out over the water, is predictably suited for terrestrials -- hoppers, ants, and I'd try a Jassid too.

Overall, there is a good fish population. Although Ensign Hollow might never be another Spring Branch, it enjoys the same protective regulations, so as more seasons pass it should only get better in terms of the size of fish.

Finding Ensign Hollow

Even more challenging than fishing the upper portion is finding the stream. The gravel road running north to Ensign is the first one you encounter that goes north (left) as you travel east from Joy Springs. It is the second road that goes north (right) if you travel west from Strawberry Point. Don't look for signs that tell you it is W67, which it really is, because all signs say St. Sebald Road. The road reverses its course once, but stay with it without taking any turns suggested by other signs pointing to St. Sebald. Just follow the straightest route you can take. You should pass, not turn onto, these roads: 345th to the left, 342nd to the right, and 338th to the right. The next left is 322nd that follows Ensign upstream.

Bloody Run

This is a long, put-and-take stream with a protected section over four miles long in the middle. There was a period when no part of the stream was protected, there were some years when the upper part was special regulation fishing, and even the lower portion was protected for a while. Of the streams discussed herein, this, at least in places, is the most like a river. Indeed, places along Bloody Run remind me in size and character of parts of Yellowstone Park's Gallatin and Gibbon Rivers. Since I've mentioned it, I'll add that the hiking involved to fish the middle portion of the stream would make a good "rehearsal" to prepare yourself for a serious fishing trip to the western states. The area is remote enough that a sprained ankle would make getting back to your car a serious ordeal. It's not a bad idea anywhere to have some matches and Band-aids in your vest.

Bloody Run also has good diversity of water; you can be fishing along in waters similar to most of our other creeks and then come upon a pool the size of a small farm pond. I recommend carrying a large fly selection and would include streamers and woolly buggers if you don't normally have them for the other streams.

Finding Bloody Run

Following U.S.18 west of MacGregor, look for the two "loops" that depart from the highway to the north and quickly rejoin it. They are sections of old highway, complete with curbs. The one closest to town, marked 145

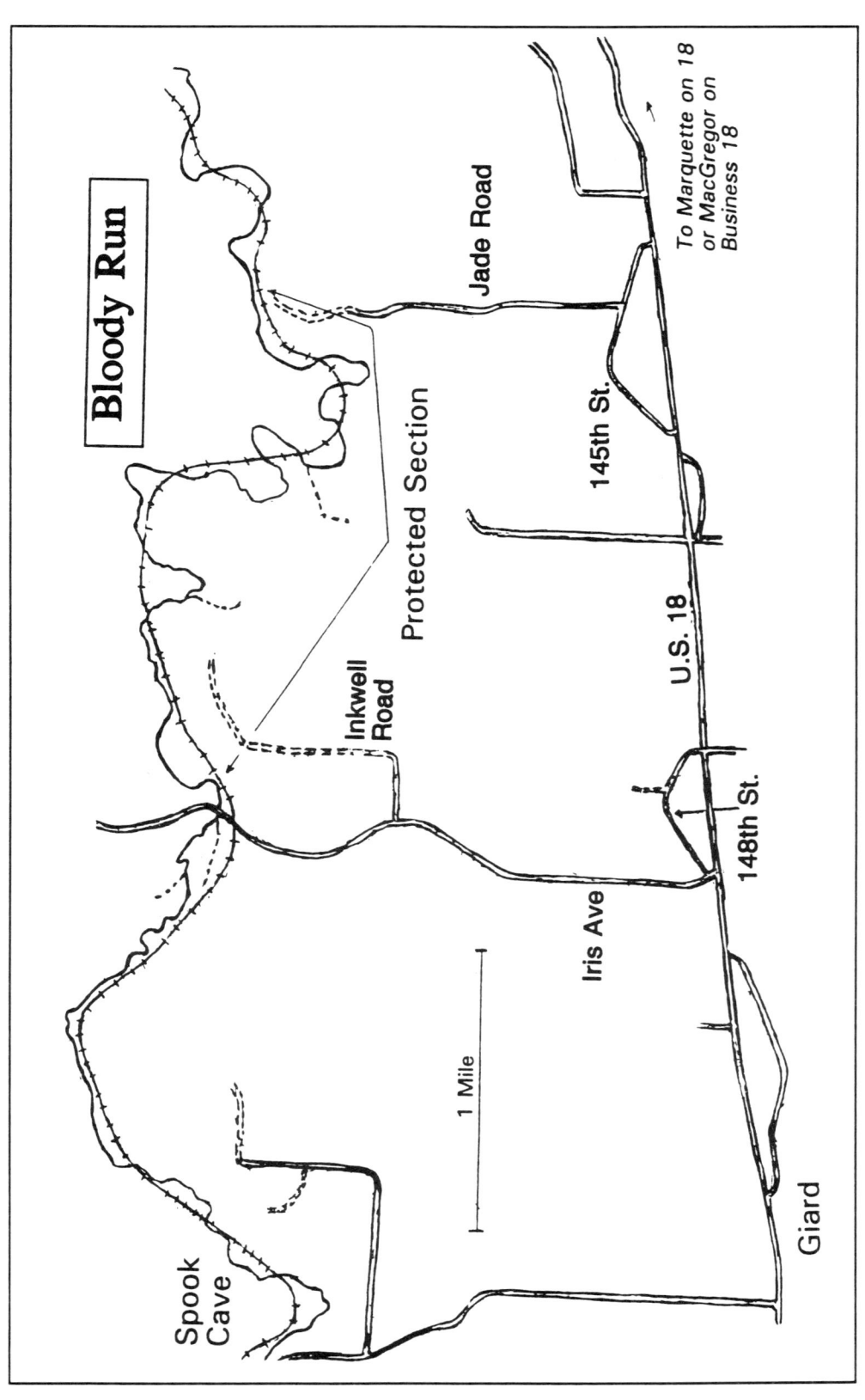

Street, is the route to the eastern end of the protected section of Bloody Run. The next loop to the west, 148th Street, is the route to the middle and western end of the protected section.

Western end and center of protected section: The gravel road at the west end of the 148th Street loop is Iris Avenue, which you follow north. Going straight takes you to a bridge across the stream near the western boundary of the special regulations area. Turning right onto Inkwell Road takes you to the middle of the protected area. Follow Inkwell as far as you dare as it curves toward the stream. The road, usable in dry seasons, deteriorates as it goes. I recommend being careful that you don't drive in while it's dry and then get stuck because of a rain storm that sets in while you are fishing.

Inkwell culminates at a gate. Walk over the rise and downhill one-half mile or so to the stream. There is protected water in both directions from here, and lots of it.

Eastern end of special regulations section: From the 145th Street loop take Jade Avenue north. Find a place to park where the road becomes Level B Service. The road passes between private lots, but is public access to the stream. From this point it is washed away to bedrock and impassable even with conventional 4-wheel drive.

Lower Bloody Run: Although not protected, there is good fishing and excellent camping at the lower end of Bloody Run. Follow U.S. 18 into Marquette and follow signs to the park.

Upper Bloody Run: Follow signs to Spook Cave. Unlike other streams, the upper reaches of Bloody Run are not the best.

South Pine

The newest experiment by the DNR folks is to see how brook trout fare in what were originally brook trout waters. This, like the upper regions of Ensign Hollow, is another tough nut to crack. In this case it is because of the amount of watercress in the stream and the amount of hiking required to get there. I'm electing here to recommend it only to seasoned anglers who have ample time and are looking for a different sort of challenge. This is the sort of stream that could suffer from publicity. Like other walk-in, put-and-grow streams, excessive fishing pressure could be its undoing.

9

The Northern Triangle

These three creeks -- Waterloo, North Bear, and French -- are the three favorite streams of veteran Iowa fly fishers. Besides their obvious relationship on the map, I've dubbed them the Northern Triangle because it is fairly common to connect all three with a single day's fishing. Any one of these streams is worth a full day (or week or even an entire season), but the temptation is always present to hop over to the next one. Maybe there will be more rising fish, or fewer anglers, or more protection from the wind, or maybe you just want to get closer to your room or camp before dark. It is true that many times you can redeem a poor day by skipping over to the next stream. To make matters even easier, there are three major towns along the base of the triangle that have good motels and restaurants. This is also one of the most beautiful parts of the state, and there are other motels and general stores off the beaten path. I mention a few of my regular haunts with the directions to the individual streams.

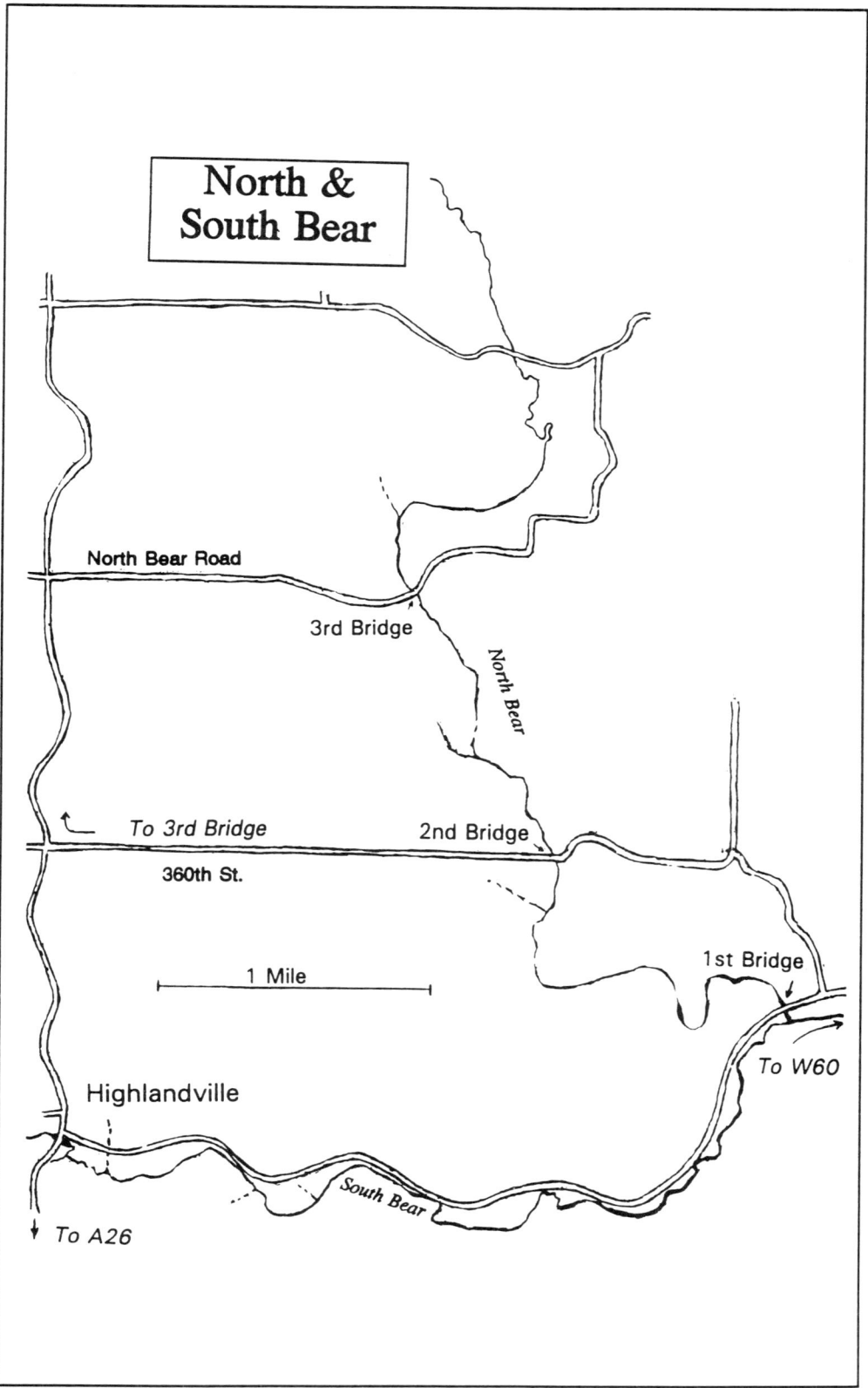

North &
South Bear

North Bear Road

3rd Bridge

North Bear

To 3rd Bridge   2nd Bridge

360th St.

1 Mile

1st Bridge

To W60

Highlandville

South Bear

To A26

North Bear

From the first bridge at its confluence with
the South Bear, you can fish the North Bear upstream nearly
to the Minnesota border. Compressed into its official
4.2-mile length is as much holding water as any other Iowa
stream I can think of. There are two more bridges with
parking areas above the first, and each has easy access to the
stream. Whether you approach from the east or west, you
are likely to first intersect the stream at the first bridge. The
section of water upward from that bridge lends itself well to
weighted Gold Ribbed Hare's Ears. As you work your way
north, be alert for rising fish as you come across flatter
water. For dry fly fishing, park at the second bridge, walk
down a mile, and fish back up. You can also work up from
the second bridge to the third, and even up from there. As I
said, there is a lot of excellent trout habitat in this stream.

I don't think I'll be giving away secrets if I say that
Ed Powell (grandson and namesake of the cane rod builder
E. C. Powell) ranks North Bear among his favorite Iowa
streams. Ed is known to fish Humpies a lot, but here he
uses an Elk Hair Caddis. He is also such a remarkable
caster that he can work almost any water with almost any fly
and catch fish if they are present. I pass this information
along as an endorsement of the stream, the fly, and
especially casting practice.

South Bear

South Bear is a fine stream that would command more attention if North Bear weren't there. Simply stated, North Bear is less accessible via road, so it gets less pressure from non-fly anglers. South Bear, with the campground and several access points, gets considerable pressure, but nonetheless is a good stream. The upper portion (above the campground) is often stocked unannounced with brown trout.

Finding North and South Bear

From Decorah, take W38, called Locust Road, toward Highlandville. At Locust, bear right onto Big Canoe Road (A26). After about 2.5 miles, just before Big Canoe Lutheran Church and the large cemetery, easily visible ahead, bear left onto Highlandville Road, which goes the remaining one mile into town. It is designated A24 on the map.

Highlandville consists of a two general stores, one immediately on your right (you probably won't see it) and then another on your left as you enter town. With the second store is a campground, and there are some houses too. Highlandville's buildings are rather scattered and it might not immediately match the mental picture you have of a "town."

Just past the second store and campground is a bridge crossing South Bear, and after that you turn right and follow South Bear Creek, now on your right, to the parking area just before the First Bridge (see description of the stream above).

The hardest part is finding W38 in Decorah. It intersects College Drive just north of the bridge crossing the Upper Iowa River off of Water Street, the main business street. There is a large convenience store there (check your gas gauge) and North Street comes in from the west.

To find this location from State Highway 9, use the map of Decorah on page 78. From the west, turning North onto U.S. 52 and then right on Fifth Avenue takes you past the city campground. From the east you can take Montgomery Street to Water Street by following signs to the business district and Luther College.

From Waterloo Creek you can get to North Bear by taking A16 west out of Dorchester and following it as it angles northwest. Turn left onto W60 going back south. The second possible turn to the right lies between two bridges, a one-lane bridge followed by a larger one. It is the road between the bridges, called the Quandahl Road, that takes you to the first bridge on North Bear.

If you are upstream from Dorchester, cross the concrete bridge (see below) going southwest and take the first left to drop down to the hard surfaced A16. From there, turn right and follow the instructions above.

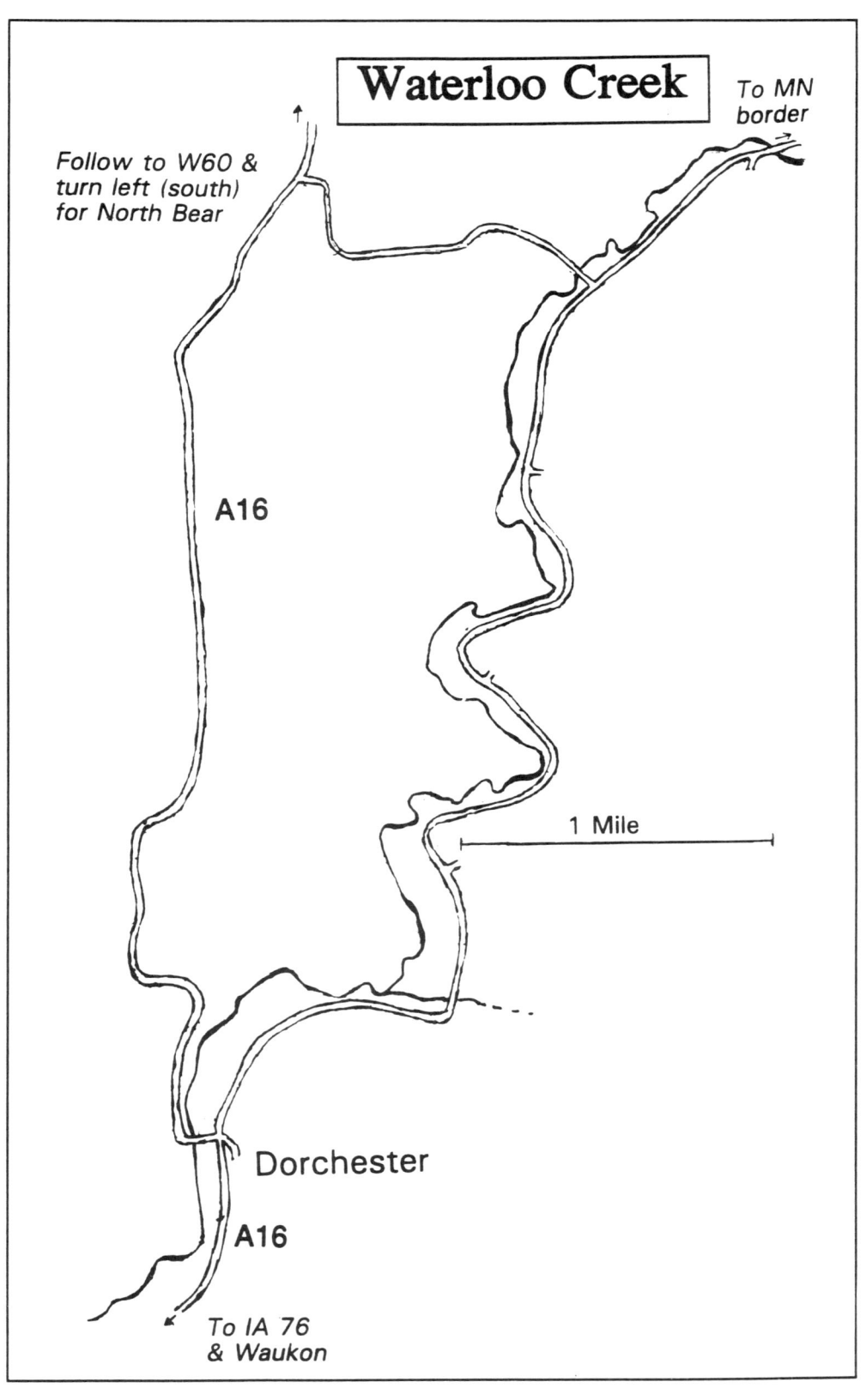

Waterloo Creek

To MN border

Follow to W60 & turn left (south) for North Bear

A16

1 Mile

Dorchester

A16

To IA 76 & Waukon

Waterloo Creek

If you see a diminutive 1966 Yellowstone travel trailer parked about ten steps from Waterloo Creek at the Pine View Campground at the western edge of Dorchester, it's mine. This is my current home-away-from-home. Not only is Waterloo Creek one of the best Iowa trout streams, it is midway between French Creek and North Bear. Via back roads, Waterloo is within 15 or 20 minutes of the two others.

To begin learning the stream, locate the three bridges: one at the south end of Dorchester, another modern concrete one about a mile from the Minnesota border, and an old, steel truss bridge almost at the border. (Across the border, Waterloo becomes Bee Creek.) Look for fish in both directions from all three bridges. Between the upper two, just before the road comes in from the right as you head upstream, is a prominent stocking hole where you will sometimes find rising fish that have eluded capture.

It seems downright criminal, but the best fishing is often where you'd rather not fish. On Colorado's famous Blue River, amid the beauty of the Rockies, the best fishing is next to the parking lot of a factory outlet mall in Silverthorn. On Waterloo Creek, in Iowa's picturesque "Little Switzerland," it is right in the middle of Dorchester.

If you don't already know how, the upper reaches of Waterloo will teach you to drift dry flies and soft hackles over holes in the watercress. Some of the sections are so delicate you have to false cast to rid your line of water droplets that would spook the fish on your next cast.

Not only here, but everywhere in the state, please release the brown trout unharmed.

Finding Waterloo Creek

This is the easiest to find of them all. Simply follow
State Highway 76 north out of Waukon and turn left on A16.
Where A16 turns left across the bridge over across the
creek, keep going straight into town. This is the first bridge
referred to above. There are crossovers to the stream on
both sides of the bridge. Dorchester has a small store and a
couple of places to eat, one of which is the Sportsman's
Motel out on the highway to Caledonia, Minnesota.

French Creek

Arguably the best stream in the state other
than Spring Branch Creek, which is in a class by itself,
French Creek is thought of in two parts, the upper portion
and the rest. There are two parking areas, and upstream
from the second one, which also serves as a primitive
campground, is the upper portion that was once protected. It is small water stocked only with brown trout and well
deserving of attention. The remaining portion of French
Creek winds from that parking site off through a valley from
which it emerges miles later at a dairy farm, and then continues under a bridge and on through pasture land.

The land from the "campground" to the dairy farm is
state owned and the vegetation grows high in the summer.
In other words, it can be tough going. My advice? Walk it.
Unlike other streams, there are not frequent bridge crossings
to make for convenient access. This, like the middle section

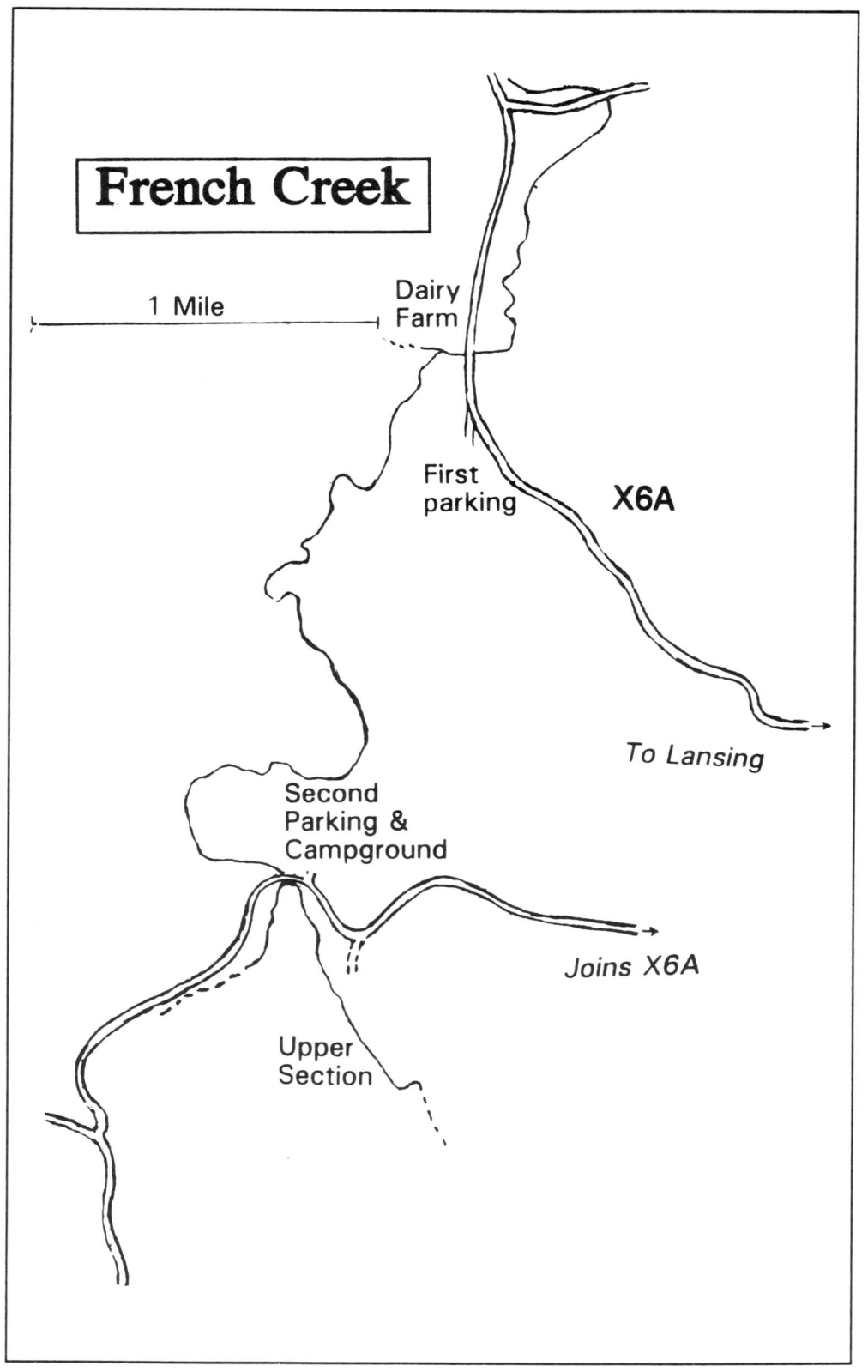

of Bloody Run, is a stream that requires effort.

Just above the farm is another parking lot. If you are working from two cars, leave one at the upper parking lot, drive down to the other and fish up, just like you would do a float trip. (The same strategy would work well at Bloody Run and North Bear.)

Finding French Creek

Find county road X6A, which goes north from State Highway 9 about two miles west of Lansing. Remain on X6A. The road will wind downhill as you approach the stream. By the time you reach the bridge where the road crosses the creek at the dairy farm, you will have missed the drive to the parking area, which cuts back hard to the left and drops out of sight. From the bridge you can fish up or down. The water immediately upstream from the bridge is good for nymph fishing.

To reach the upper parking and camping area from here, take X6A back toward Lansing and turn right at the first opportunity. Go straight, and when you reach bottom land the road will turn right while a lane continues straight. Turning to the right takes you to the upper parking lot, while going straight takes you to a separate parking area for fishing the upper stream.

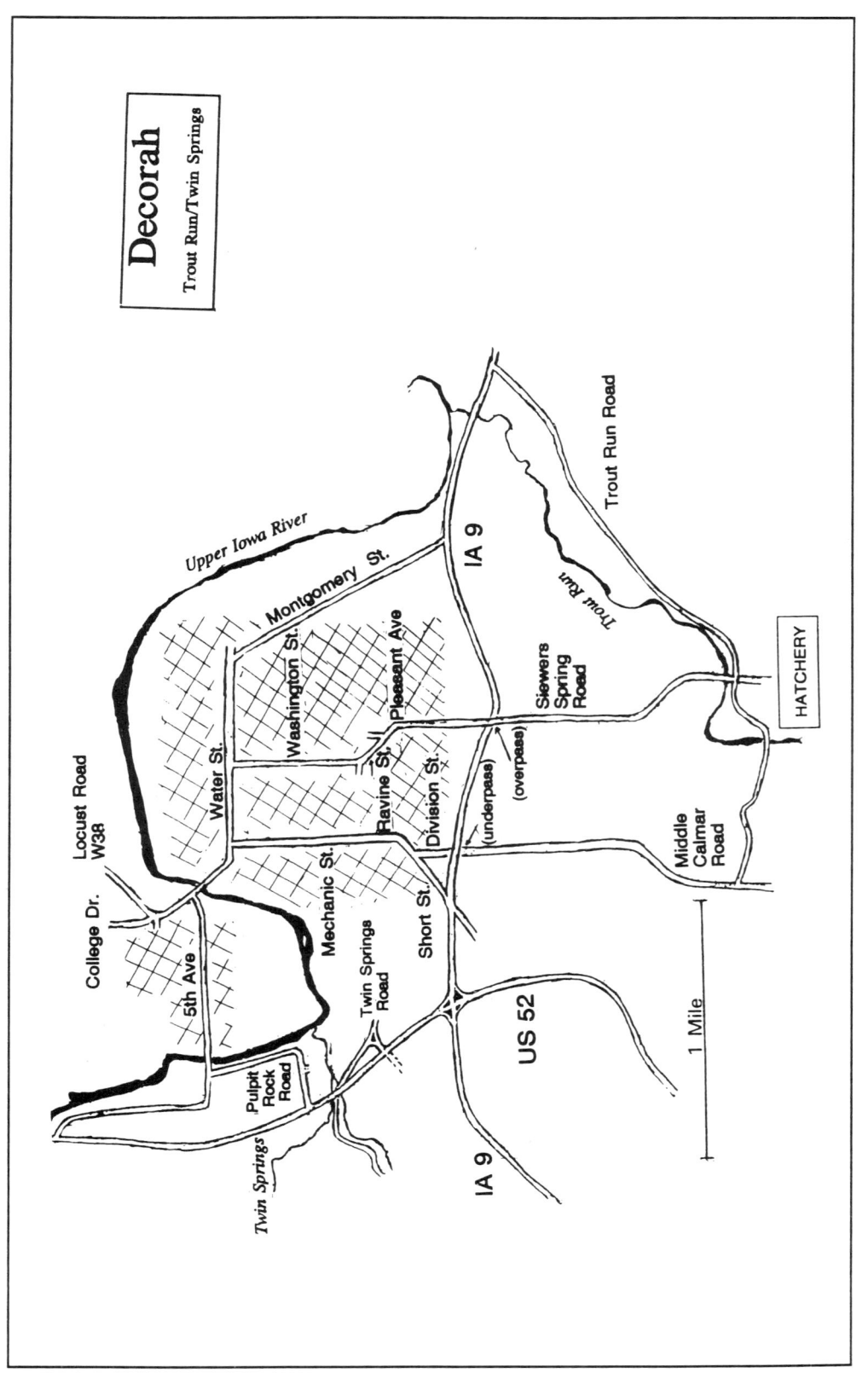

10

Decorah

If there is a "heart" of Iowa trout country it is Decorah. That is not to detract from Lansing and Waukon, or even Dorchester and Highlandville, as good bases of operation, but for a first visit to the area, Decorah is ideally situated. The drive to Highlandville is only about one-half hour. To Lansing is roughly an hour. For a dry fly angler who waits until midmorning to begin, breakfast at the Clarksville Diner is outstanding. As diners go, this one ranks right up there with the celebrated Moody's Diner on Maine's Route 1.

The map is included here because it is inevitable that someone seriously fishing Iowa streams will need to find his or her way through Decorah. The streams, although somewhat a by-product of the street map, are still worthy of mention.

Trout Run

As with the hatchery at Spring Branch Creek, allow time to walk through the rearing station when you visit here. You can't miss it, but take special notice of the decorative water falls at Siewers Spring. To fish Trout Run I recommend driving back down Trout Run Road toward State Highway 9 and parking at the spot near the remains of the railroad trestle. Fish both up and down, way down, from there.

Twin Springs

This stream is heavily fished because of the campground, but as a rule it is heavily stocked. As I said at the beginning of this section, you might not go out of your way to fish here, but the combination of a decent stream with a good camp site is fine indeed. Upstream you will encounter original runs of an historic hatchery that was here.

Finding Trout Run
and Twin Springs

Refer to the map for both streams. Get to Twin Springs most easily from Twin Springs Road, not from the campground. For your first visit to Trout Run, look for the intersection of Trout Run Road with route 9 on the western edge of town. Returning to town via Siewer's Spring Road or Middle Calmar Road will help you learn these shorter but harder-to-find routes from town.

11

South of Decorah

From the many streams in the more central region of trout country I have included the three below based not only on relative popularity, but also on size and diversity. Both Sny Magill and Otter are large creeks with ample length for fish and anglers, and they both have smaller branches, North Cedar and Glover's respectively, that offer additional, smaller-stream opportunities.

Sny Magill and North Cedar

Easy to find and to fish, with numerous parking spots, Sny Magill, like Big Mill discussed below, receives heavy pressure from the general angling public. There is, however, plenty of water to work between stocking holes, and the stretch of North Cedar upstream from Sny is less accessible and offers comparative solitude. Sny Magill

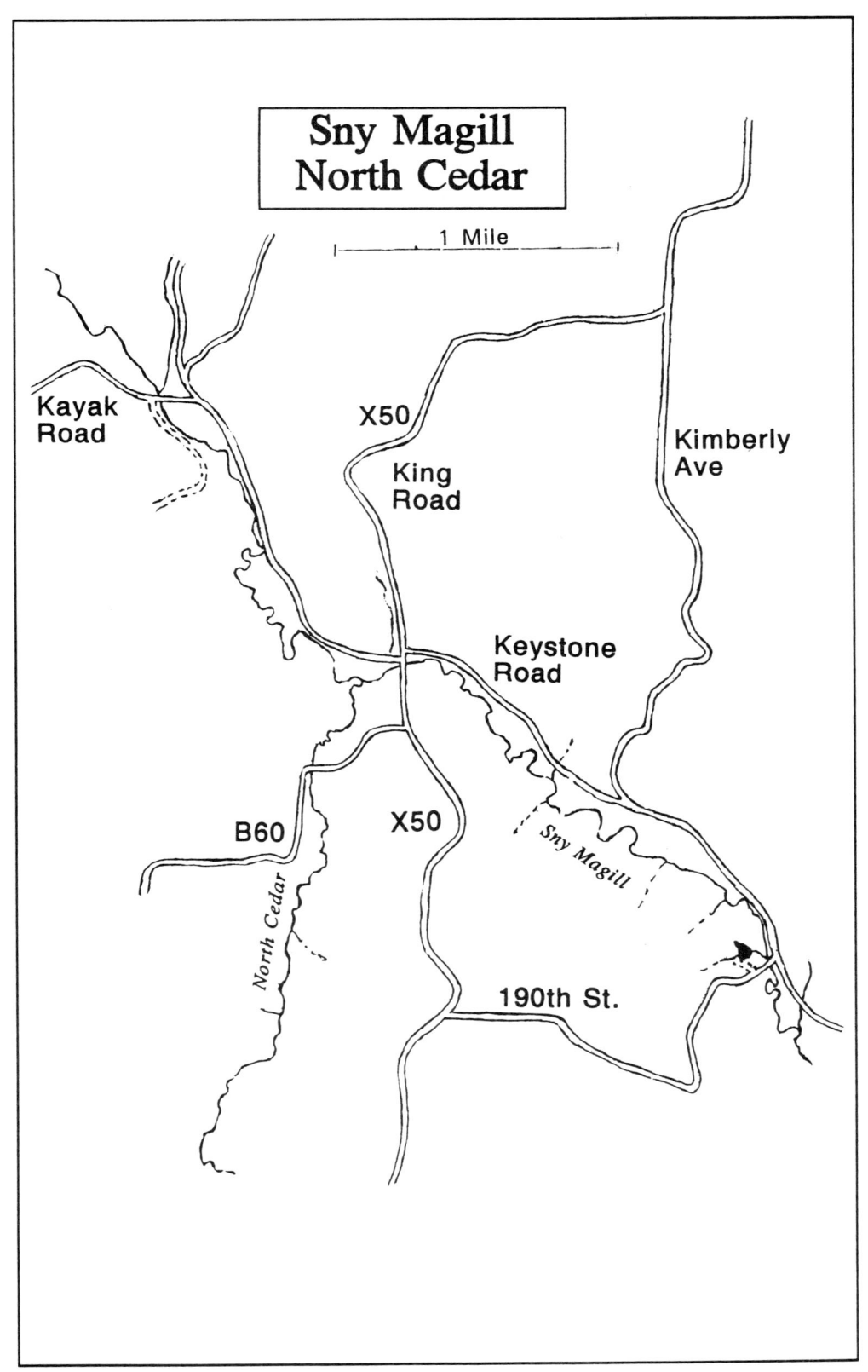

Sny Magill
North Cedar

1 Mile

Kayak Road

X50

King Road

Kimberly Ave

Keystone Road

B60

X50

North Cedar

Sny Magill

190th St.

has been known to produce some exceptionally large browns. This is a stream where I would keep a critical eye on the insect activity and try woolly worms and streamers if the action is slow. Terrestrials too should be good producers when in season. I recommend working the upstream portion first and immediately before dark checking the larger, downstream pools.

Finding Sny Magill and North Cedar

From either U.S. 52 or State Highway 13 take B60 -- also called Ivory Road -- to the east. Turn left on X50 -- King Road -- and directly in front of you is a bridge with a parking area on the right. This puts you in the center of the map.

From MacGregor follow Business 18 out of town (away from the river) and watch for X50, which comes in from the left and follow it to the stream.

Otter and Glover's

Unlike Sny Magill and North Cedar, these streams are generally not fished at the same time, although they could be. The confluence of the two streams, located a substantial distance from any road access, is one of the many spots I hope to explore someday. Glover's is a lovely, small pastureland stream that carries over some fish through the winter. There is one run through the pasture that has abundant watercress, which translates to abundant cover

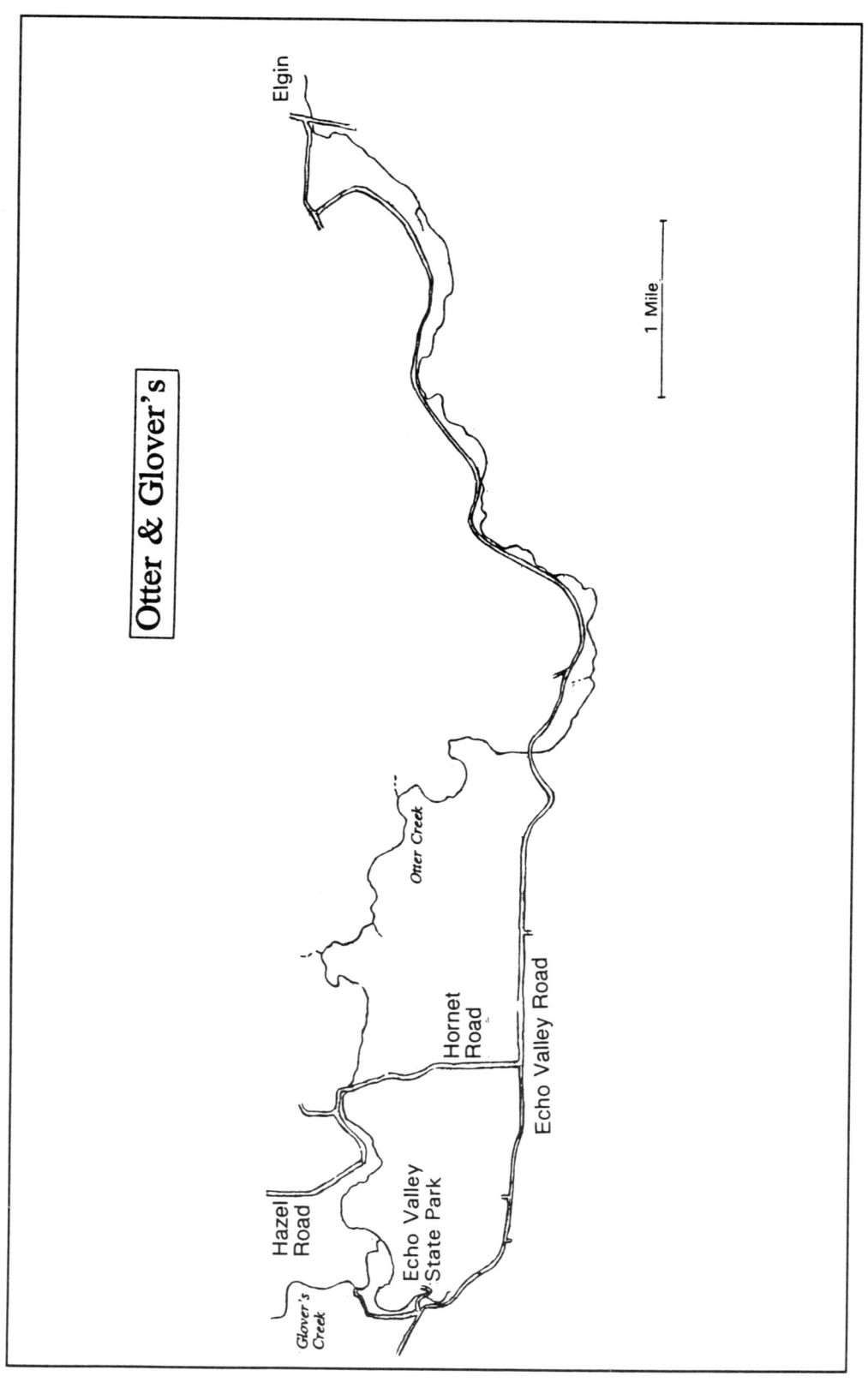

Otter & Glover's

Elgin

1 Mile

Otter Creek

Glover's
Creek

Hazel
Road

Echo Valley
State Park

Hornet
Road

Echo Valley Road

where trout can avoid anglers when the pressure is on. This, like so many places, would be one to check out in the final moments of daylight.

Otter Creek, on the other hand, is a hefty piece of water that has a little bit of everything. The trout waters start at the dramatic cliffs in Echo Valley State Park and run more than nine miles to the town of Elgin. As you enter the park, it is the water to your left that holds fish. From Elgin back upstream the creek follows the Echo Valley Road, then crosses under it at an old steel bridge and disappears to the north. The next access is reached by following the road and turning right on Hornet Road, which descends to a concrete bridge that crosses Otter. Fish both up and down from here. Like many streams, I recommend concentrating flyfishing efforts first on the upper, faster waters and carrying streamers and wooly worms for the slower, deeper sections.

Finding Glover's and Otter

To reach Echo Valley Road and the park from West Union, proceed east (toward town) on State Highway 18 from its intersection with State Highway 150. At the second traffic signal, just past the ball field, turn right onto Pine Street (Pine Street to the left is county road W42). Follow Pine downhill and bear left at the foot of the hill where there is an apartment building on the right. This is Echo Valley Road, and the entrance to the park is on the left, 1.7 miles ahead. Immediately upon turning you can either turn left again to reach the parking area at Glover's, or take the right fork down into the park. If you do not enter the park, Echo

Valley Road becomes gravel and proceeds past Hornet Road and on to Elgin.

The other route you need to know is the one from West Union to the concrete bridge on Hornet described above. For this route you continue east through town on 18 and turn right on B64 (Golden Road) at the point where 18 curves northeastward. Take the first right turn onto Hazel Road, and it will take you to the concrete bridge where Hornet and Hazel Roads meet.

In Elgin, which is connected to West Union by both Echo Valley Road and Golden Road (B64), the bridge over Otter Creek is just south of the water tower. If you follow Echo Valley Road along the stream and continue straight instead of turning on Hornet Road as described above, you will reach the entrance to the park (now on your right), just where the gravel turns to pavement.

12

Backbone Area

Backbone State Park, one of the most striking in the state, can be the focal point of both fine angling and a relaxing family vacation. This area is also reasonably close to Manchester and Spring Branch Creek.

Richmond Springs

Richmond Springs, the best of the three streams included here, has excellent numbers of trout. During the winter, when the park is closed, the stream is still reachable on foot, and large numbers of resident rainbows have been known to be caught. I recommend releasing winter rainbows to perpetuate the quality of this off-season fishery. The park's managers may modify the

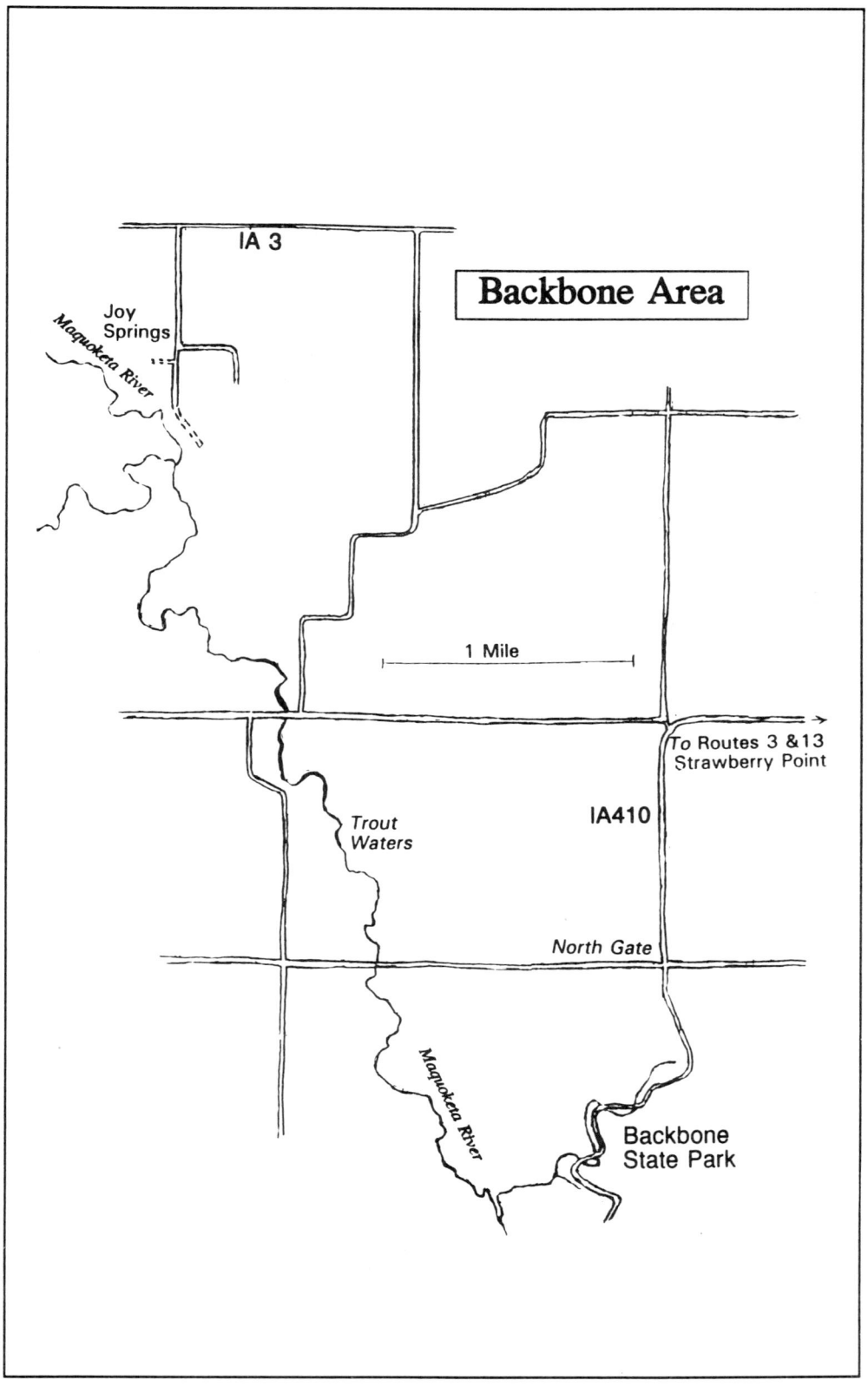

season somewhat depending on the weather, but figure that the park roads close on November 15 and reopen on April 15. To walk from the north entrance to the upper reaches of the stream is about one-half mile.

For some reason unknown to me, Richmond Springs trout have a healthy appetite for wooly worm patterns, especially tied in black. The wooly worm is always an effective trout pattern, especially when tied as small as a #14, but in this stream the larger sizes seem to work well.

Finding Richmond Springs

Backbone State Park has four main entrances, and it is the North Gate that is closest to Richmond Springs. To get to the North Gate, use State Highway 410 which begins at the intersection of State Highways 3 and 13 outside Strawberry Point. From that intersection, 410 goes west for one mile and then curves south into the North Gate.

Once inside the park, the stream first comes into sight on your right as you descend to the bridge and first picnic area. After following the road and then crossing it four times, the stream departs to the right. There is a long stretch of stream, from where it leaves the road to its confluence with the Maquoketa River, that can be reached only on foot.

When you approach from the West Gate and descend the hill you must turn left, past the shelters, and follow that road to Balanced Rock, which is directly over one of Richmond Springs' good pools (good in normal or wet seasons, I should say). From the West Gate the first water you see is the Maquoketa River, not Richmond Springs.

The Maquoketa is also a designated trout stream, but the best fishing is above the park. If you fail to make the left turn toward Richmond Springs, the road crosses the Maquoketa just past a sign indicating "Trout Waters." Don't let this sign confuse you. Richmond Springs is about a mile away.

On the eastern side of the park there are two entrances, both clearly marked as you go north on county road W69. It is the one farthest north, the East Gate off of route C57, that you want. (C57 intersects W69 from the west.) From this entrance proceed past the park office to the Maquoketa River crossing described above. At the park office are complimentary large-scale maps that will help you find your way through the park.

Joy Springs and the Maquoketa

Joy Springs was discussed at the beginning of this section. It is a great little park and the trout waters there (really the Maquoketa River) are decent, although there isn't a lot of holding water for resident fish. The section of the Maquoketa between Joy Springs and Backbone, however, has potential. It is stocked mainly with brown trout.

Finding Joy Springs and The Maquoketa

Joy Springs is a well-marked turnoff from State Highway 3, and the section of the Maquoketa to fish begins at the bridge due west of the North Gate of the park and continues up to the next bridge to the north.

13

Swiss Valley

This easy-to-find stream, which on the state's map is identified as "Upper and Lower Swiss Valley," has sufficient length to provide a variety of trout habitat, and it is served by a large modern campground, a nice park, and a nature center with displays, restrooms, and hiking trails. This offers a fine blend of fishing and family vacationing. The area is lovely and interesting, the fishing is very respectable.

Upstream from the nature center, the upper reaches of the stream (called Catfish Creek on topographical maps) were protected by special regulations for a couple of seasons and hold good-sized fish, but large fish have also been recorded from the lower section at the campground. I've caught nice fish from the middle portion simply by prospecting with an Orange Governor, one of the classic wet flies I tie. Terrestrials produce well here in the summer months. The official designation of Upper Swiss begins where the service road above the nature center crosses the stream. It is

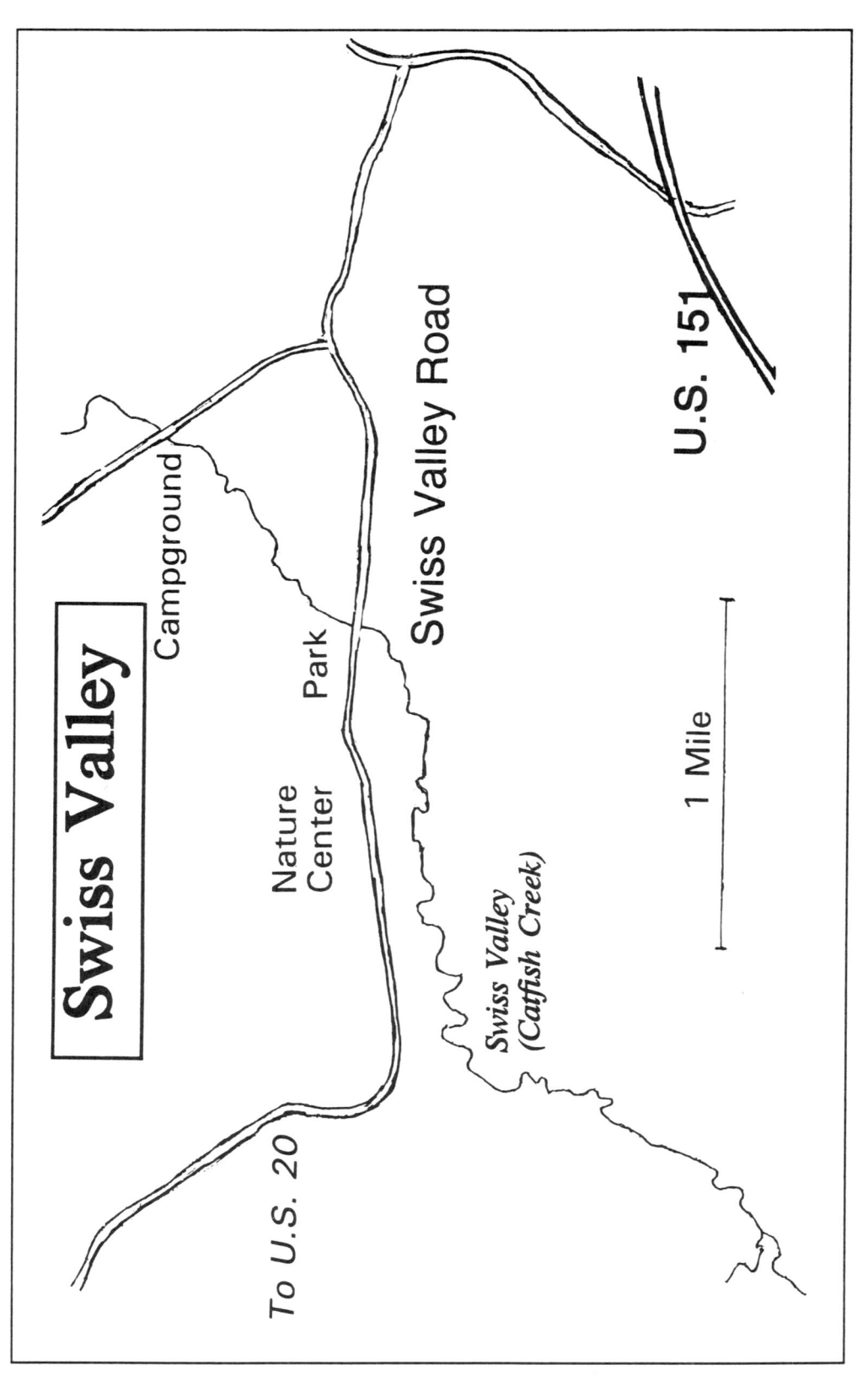

Swiss Valley

Campground

Nature
Center

Park

Swiss Valley Road

To U.S. 20

Swiss Valley
(Catfish Creek)

U.S. 151

1 Mile

upstream from there that fly anglers can expect the best action.

Finding Swiss Valley

Following U.S. 20 from the west, Swiss Valley is about 33 miles from Manchester. Well marked with brown and yellow signs directing you to Swiss Valley, the road, Swiss Valley Road, turns off of 20 to the right as you reach the outskirts of Dubuque where 20 bends northeast toward Dubuque proper. Alternately, the other end of this road is reached from U.S. 151 as it leaves Dubuque. From Dubuque you follow 151, and stay to the right where U.S. 61 branches off to the left. There is a brown and white Conservation Commission sign indicating the right turn toward Swiss Valley. Follow that road for about a mile and another sign will direct you to the left onto Swiss Valley Road. From this direction you reach the turnoff to the Campground first, followed by the park at the bridge and then the nature center.

14

The Southern Streams

Of the three streams off to themselves at the southern extremity of trout country, Big and Little Mill and Brush Creek, each is unique and has a different kind of appeal.

Big Mill

Big Mill, primarily stocked with rainbow trout, is indeed the larger of the two creeks by that name. It and Little Mill join forces just after they cross under State Highway 62, which is just before they fall into the Mississippi River. The fact that it is the larger simply means that Big Mill has longer, wider pools, and from a flyfishing point of view that merely means greater popularity with bait fishers. Remember also that these streams are the closest ones for the numerous anglers from the Davenport area (the "Quad Cities").

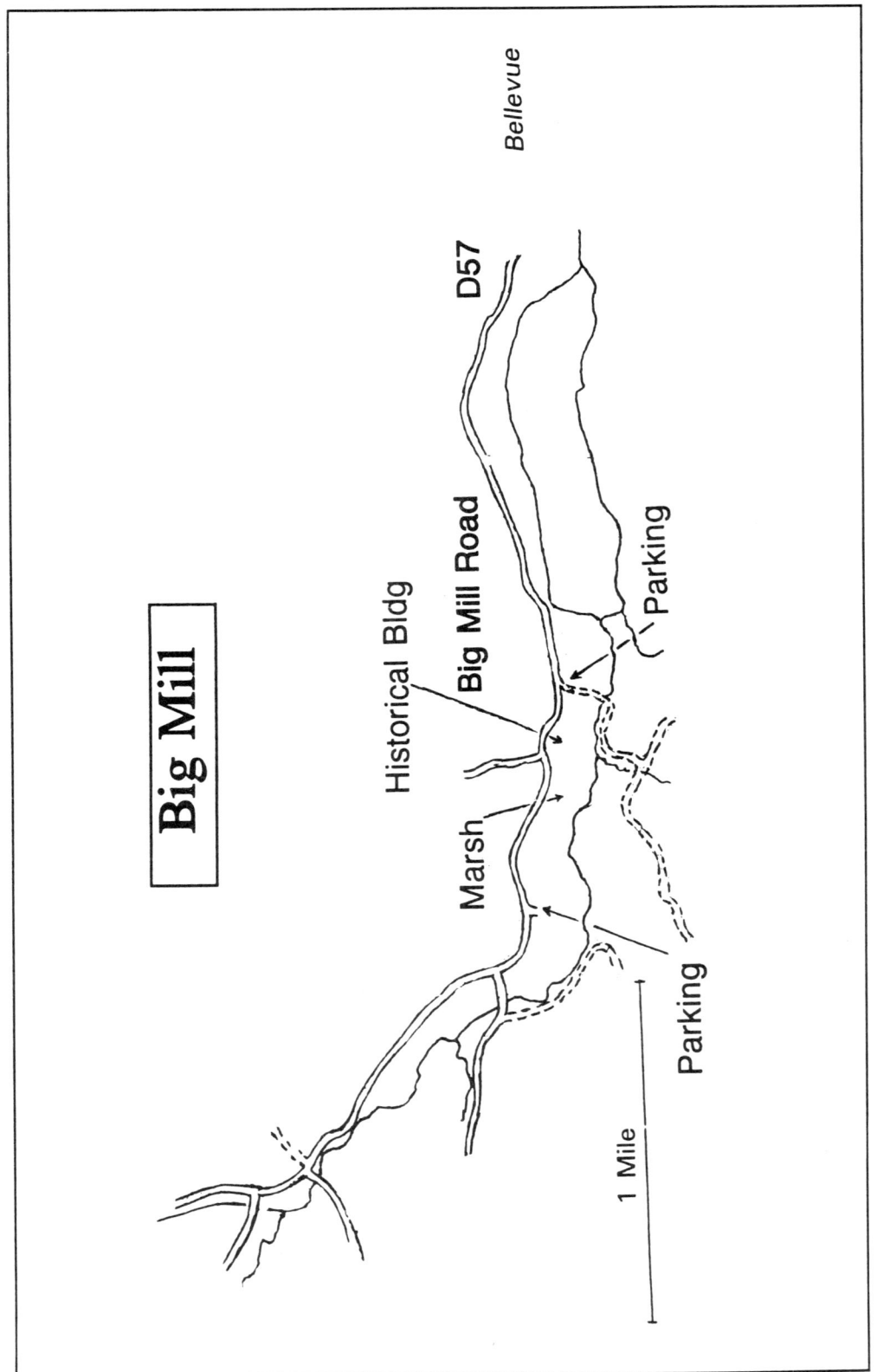

Big Mill

In addition to following the advice I've already given on dealing with fishing pressure, there is one other tip that will help, and it relates directly to the character of the stream itself.

Big Mill, at least the stocked portion of it, is a succession of large, slow pools, and it is into these pools that the stocking trucks unceremoniously deposit their cargo, so it is there that the bobber anglers concentrate their efforts. But even on the most crowded Saturday morning I have found rising fish (and comparative solitude) by looking for fast narrow runs or deep riffles between the pools. When you do find a fish in this situation, take your time and enjoy working him. Change flies often, seine the water for bug samples, rest the spot frequently, see what his rises look like, etc.

The bottom of the stream is clay and can be very slippery. I recommend lug soled wading shoes rather than felt soled ones. If you are approaching fish in one of the pools, wade slowly and carefully so as not to send waves of muddy water ahead of you.

The portion of Big Mill that is stocked is relatively short, and the two parking areas are only one-half mile apart. These parking areas also provide access to public land for hunters and hikers and such, so all the cars you see won't necessarily belong to anglers. The best flyfishing water is behind the marsh and upstream a little.

Finding Big Mill

If you are traveling on Route 62, which is State Street in Bellevue, turn north (left when driving toward the

Mississippi) on Seventh Street, and in a couple of blocks you will hit a 5-way stop. Take the road that bears left (not the hard left) and you will be on Mill Creek Road, also known as county road D57. This is the road you want, but be careful to stay on it. Almost immediately the road divides, with paved road curving uphill to the right while D57 changes abruptly to gravel. You want to go straight on the gravel for 4.3 miles.

No matter how hard you try, you will miss the first parking area for the simple reason that the drive is invisible until you are past it. Once you have passed it you should see the parking area on your left and you can go back to it. But if you don't, you'll almost immediately see the Big Mill Homestead maintained by the local historical society.

Following the historical society building there is a marsh and then the second parking area, which is almost exactly one-half mile from the first.

If you are traveling on U.S. 52 through Bellevue, D57 butts right into it. D57 is also called Park Street. Route 52 occupies the place where First Street should be, but they liked the sound of "Riverview" better. So U.S. 52 is Riverview, and Second, Third, etc. run parallel to it. Don't worry, you can't get lost in Bellevue anyway.

There is a motel on the Northern outskirts of town, and there is the Riverview Hotel-Cafe-Bar right at the junction of State (Rt. 62) and Riverview (Rt. 52). It has loads of character, which usually means dirt, but in this case means truly classy rooms, some of which allow you to watch the sun rise over Lock and Dam No. 12 on the Mississippi River. Antique furniture, complete with real crocheted doilies under porcelain dishes holding herbs and stuff make it like a bed-and-breakfast, but less costly and with a down-home cafe and lively bar downstairs.

Little Mill

It stands to reason, I think, that this narrower edition of Big Mill runs a little quicker, which means a couple of things. First, there seems to be less sediment, and second, there are more agreeable places for trout to hang out. The DNR apparently agrees, because the stream has benefited from some habitat improvement and is stocked primarily with brown trout. Although the two streams are accessed via different roads (this is closer to town), it is still easy to investigate them both. For flyfishing, though, I like Little Mill much better. If I were stopping over in the neighborhood with only limited fishing time, this would be my choice over Big Mill or Brush Creek.

Like all of the diminutive streams, it's easy to frighten fish before getting a chance to cast to them. The riffles below pools are the places to look first for fish here, so be wary when approaching pools from downstream. Often there will be a fish or two in the first couple of feet of riffle below the pool (tail water). With a normal length leader you should be able to put your fly a couple of feet into the pool and still have the butt of it behind the fish. Be ready. The water moves fast at the tail, and the fish must strike quickly to get your offering.

The pools here are smaller and not as likely to get pounded by bait anglers. In all, Little Mill is my current favorite of the Southern streams.

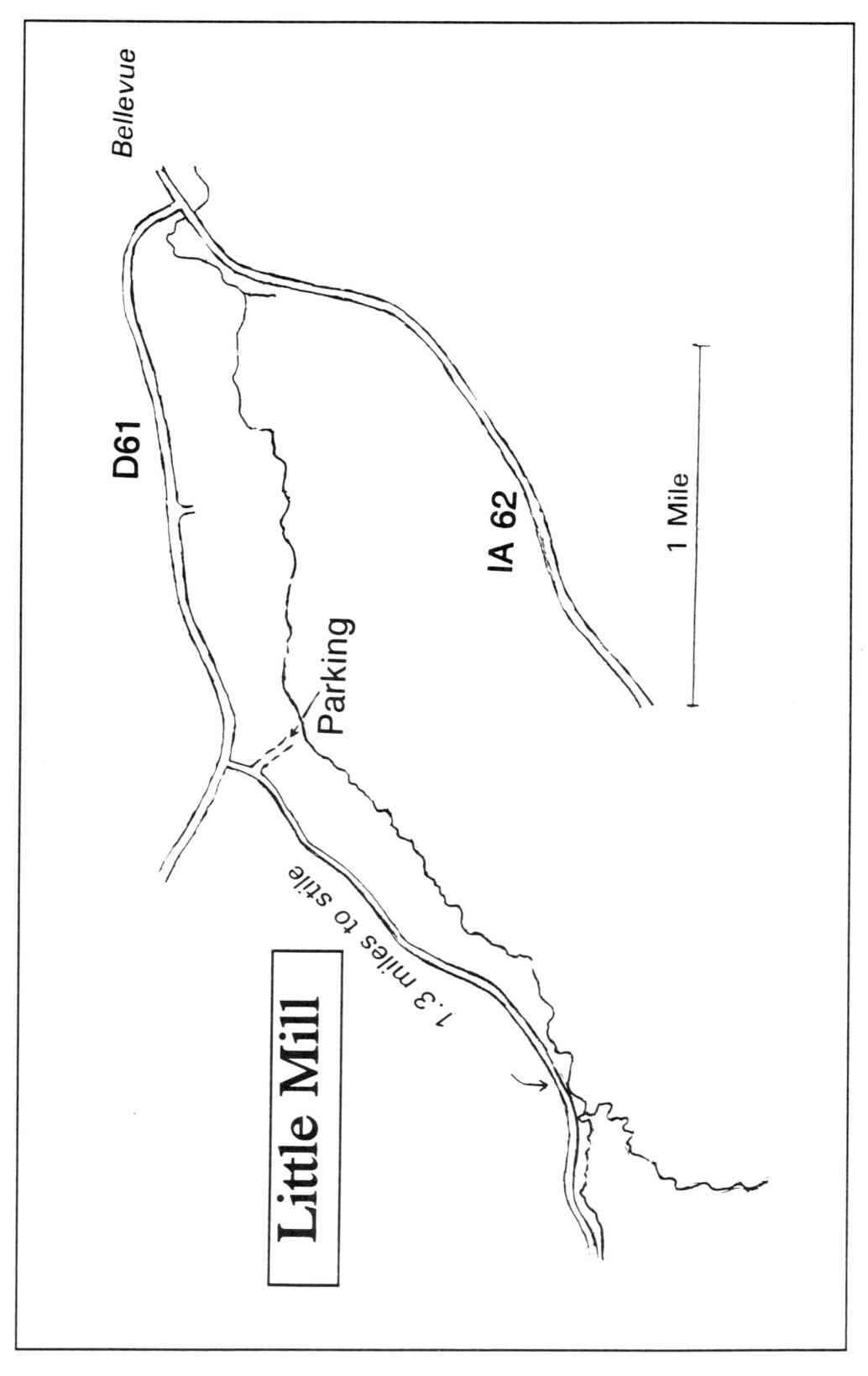

Little Mill

1.3 miles to stile

Parking

D61

IA 62

Bellevue

1 Mile

Finding Little Mill

There is a description of the Bellevue street layout and the town's amenities above. Little Mill is accessed from D61, called Bellevue Cascade Road, which butts into State Highway 62 (State Street) at the edge of town, just west of the school. (Because everything in town runs parallel to the river, northbound streets run northwest, and the westbound streets perpendicular to them actually run southwest.) Follow Bellevue Cascade Road 1.6 miles and turn left onto the gravel road that parallels the stream. You can take another left almost immediately and be at the first parking area, or you can proceed another 1.3 miles and find a stile over the fence that leads to the stream.

Brush Creek

Brush Creek, the southernmost of all the Iowa trout streams, is characterized by long slow pools meandering through pasture land. Most of the commentary on Big Mill is applicable to Brush, except that for a beginning caster, this stream is as easy as they get. Again, look for fish around fast moving water.

Although there doesn't appear to be a great deal of good holding water, I have seen brown trout going through their mating antics there. It's doubtful that the neighborhood is the greatest for raising kids, but I know that those par-

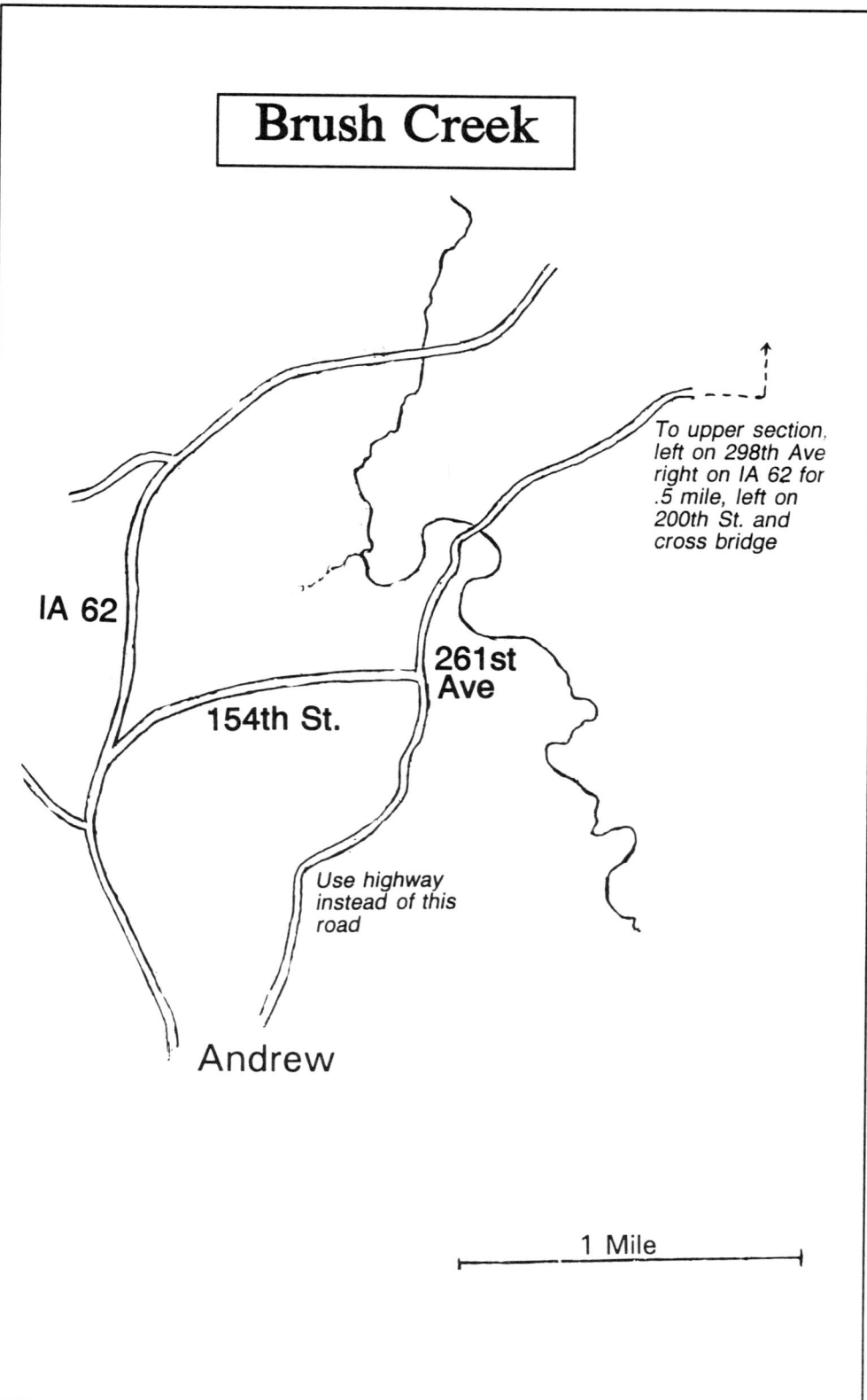

Brush Creek

IA 62

154th St.

261st
Ave

To upper section,
left on 298th Ave
right on IA 62 for
.5 mile, left on
200th St. and
cross bridge

Use highway
instead of this
road

Andrew

1 Mile

ticular fish eluded capture for awhile. In all, the stream probably sustains a few resident fish, and the location is lovely. While not a stream to stake your hopes on for a serious flyfishing adventure, it would be an excellent place to teach kids or friends how to fish. For that I would be tempted to be there on stocking day.

Finding Brush Creek

On the map it looks as though two roads out of Andrew lead to the stream. In fact, one of them deteriorates into a Level B Service road. To get to the creek easily, follow State Highway 62 northerly through Andrew and take the first right on the gravel road marked 154th Street. Turn left when it butts into another gravel road, 261st Avenue, and as it winds downhill the old steel bridge at the base of an impressive limestone cliff will come into view. Park at the crossover there and fish the designated waters downstream.

On the map you will also see a short section of the creek upstream from here. To get there, proceed on across the bridge and follow road until it hits 298th Avenue, where you turn left to return to route 62. Turn right, away from Andrew, and go one-half mile to 200th Street (it's right next to a house, so don't overlook it thinking it is a driveway). Follow 200th. It will cross a bridge, and the short section of stream will be on your left, obvious because of crossovers.

Part III

Reflections

15

Streams in Retrospect

I arrived at this point in the text through a process that involved fishing, writing, fishing some more, drawing the maps, fishing some more, researching the details, fishing some more, taking the photos, fishing some more, and so forth. In one month alone I fished 18 streams. During all of those "fishing some more" episodes I noticed things that I want to emphasize.

Without being conscious that I was doing it, whether I was driving or taking pictures or fishing, I spent each day in trout country deciding where I wanted to fish at dark. I was enjoying a particularly nice afternoon at Glover's, and as the sun started sinking I noticed I'd begun hurrying. Without it ever forming as a concrete thought, at some point during the day I had decided that at dark I wanted to be at the middle bridge on Otter Creek. Once there, I caught and saw the best fish of the day.

Another thing I noticed was that my fly selection is geared toward streams that I fish regularly, like Spring Branch Creek and French Creek, that have healthy populations of aquatic insects. Not all streams do, and from now on there will be more streamers and Woolly Worms with me, probably a whole box of them. They'll also work well on all streams during the early hours before the morning hatches start coming off. In case you don't know it, I'll add here that there are monster browns that can only be caught after dark, usually on streamers.

Another thing that I mentioned earlier that deserves reiteration is the importance of walking, especially on your first visit to a stream. For fly anglers, the upper reaches of the streams, where the water is cleaner and quicker, are often the best. If you can, resist the temptation to start fishing at the first fishable water you encounter.

In the preceding pages I've tried to err on the side of optimism, and while visiting new streams and revisiting familiar ones I found that I'm more enthused than ever about Iowa trout fishing. I have a long list of new places where I want to spend some serious days fishing.

My son Jesse, mentioned in the introduction, was right. Not only are there lots of fish out there, there are some big fish out there. While walking one section of stream, rod under my arm, I saw an exceptionally nice brown feeding in the rocks. I was leisurely tying on a nymph to show to him when just 20 feet away, on the upstream side of a small rock, a two-foot brown porpoised so slowly and deliberately that I could count his spots. The memory is a little chilling, but I swear he looked me in the eye. By the time I changed to a different fly I had buck fever so badly I put my first backcast in the weeds, freed it, and then promptly put my first forward cast in some branches hanging out over the rock.

That doesn't happen to me usually, like when I'm out west where truly large fish are more common. The point is, try to be mentally prepared for large fish when you find them, which will be more often than you expect, yet not often enough to be commonplace.

16

Loose Ends

As you might imagine, during the concentrated fishing I did just before bringing this to print, I tied hundreds of knots, and at the same time I realized that they are too important to overlook in these pages. If you struggle with knots, they become expensive in terms of lost fish and incurred frustration. Equally expensive are the ones we don't tie when we should -- the tippet that needs to be lengthened, the heavier tippet that we need to turn over a larger fly, the fly that should be retied after catching a few fish, the wind knots we ignore.

I have been circulating a booklet I wrote on knots for some time now, and on the first page I point out what I consider to be a great truth: There are only three knots you really need to know on the water, but the time that you need them most is right at dark with the wind hammering your face and your waders full of ice water. That's the time you'll break off your fly just as you spot a trophy fish rising. The knots you need, you need to tie swiftly and correctly without having to think.

If you have a permanent loop on your fly line and

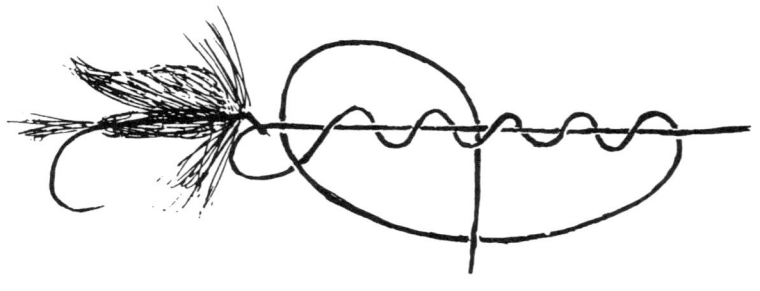

spend your evenings at home rebuilding used leaders so you'll always have one ready, the number of on-the-water knots drops to zero.

There are always new knots to try, and although I'm handy with knots and learn new ones easily, the three I rely on most are ones I've used for years and years. The terminology in the following instructions has nautical roots -- the "tag" end is the portion you will eventually trim away, and the "standing portion" is the part that remains attached to something.

Begin with an eye toward craftsmanship. Speed will come with time. One of the most common mistakes I see is people not allowing enough tag end when they start a knot.

The Improved Clinch Knot

This is the old standby that most people already use for tying on hooks.

Steps in tying the Improved Clinch Knot:

Pass the line through the hook as shown, and wrap the tag end around the standing line 5 times. This creates a loop at the hook eye.

Pass the tag end through the new loop. Doing so creates another open loop, and you pass the tag end back through that.

Moisten the knot as you tighten it.

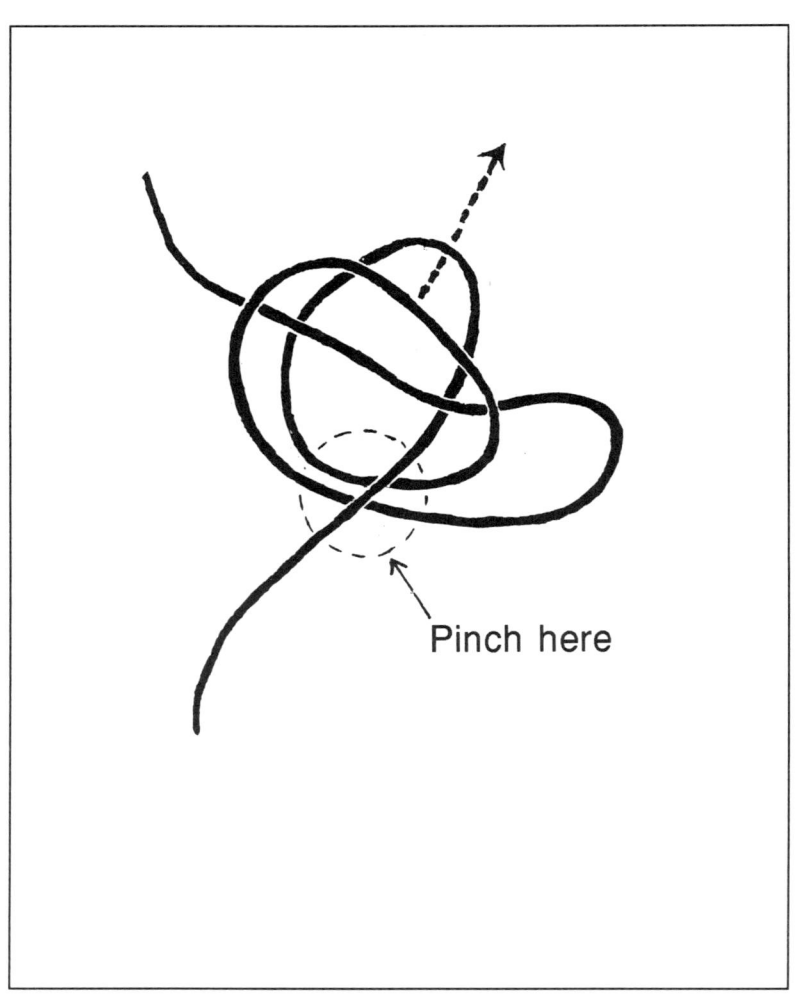

Pinch here

The Perfection Loop

This is the one knot for which I know of no acceptable substitute. I use it on the permanent leader butt that is attached to the flyline and on the butt of every leader. It's a "must learn" knot. Don't skimp on the amount you leave for the tag end. Start out by practicing it big and then gradually work smaller and smaller until you can tie a really small one.

Steps in tying the Perfection Loop:

Form a loop with the tag end passing behind the standing portion (hold it by pinching it between your thumb and forefinger where the lines cross, and leave the tag end fairly long).

Continuing in the same direction, form a second, somewhat smaller loop by bringing the tag end in front of the first loop and then around the back. You should now be pinching both loops.

Fold the tag end back over and nestle it down between the two loops (you have to hold it with the same hand that is pinching the loops).

Finally, from the back, reach through the first loop, take hold of the second, smaller loop, and pull it backward, out through the first loop. Keep a good hold on everything as you initially tighten the finished Perfection Loop, and for final tightening insert a pencil or other tool through the loop and give the standing end a good tug.

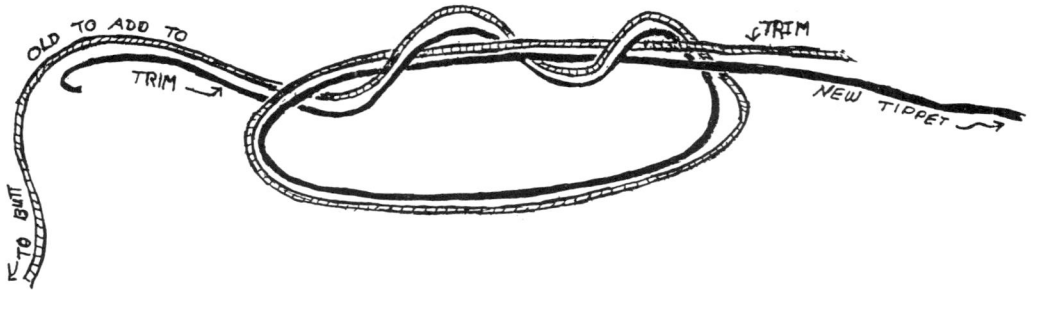

The Double Surgeon's Knot

This is a good, easily tied knot for adding new tippet, and most people find it easier to tie than the traditional Blood Knot.

Steps in tying the Double Surgeon's Knot:

Overlap the two tag ends and, treating them as a single piece, tie an overhand knot, but then bring the two pieces of the free end through the loop a second time.

Moisten the knot as you tighten it.

Traveling Tip

It isn't a knot, but I included here a good tip for securing your fly and leader while you walk or drive around. By bringing the leader down under the reel seat and back up along the rod, you can hook the fly in any nearby snake guide. This allows you to leave an ample portion of the flyline itself outside the tip of the rod so it will be ready to use quickly when you start fishing again. When you try this you will see that if you need a little more slack because the fly is a little short of reaching the next guide, you just grab the line from the reel between any two snake guides and pull a little more from the reel, moving it toward the tip (the same direction you need to move the fly).

17

A Fable

Remember fables? Like *The Hare and the Tortoise* and *The Fox and the Crow*? Here is one I want to leave with you. I heard it told by a bartender to a tourist who was grumbling about the "flyfishing only" restriction on the Railroad Ranch portion of the Henry's Fork. That section of the river was passed on from railroad tycoon E. H. Harriman to his sons and eventually to the State of Idaho. Roland Harriman was the one who loved and managed the river. The tourist couldn't understand why he wasn't allowed to at least use artificial lures with his spinning rod. The bartender explained it this way:

"For years Mister Harriman allowed everyone to fish on the river through his property, and for years Mister Harriman watched other fishermen trash the stream side while flyfishers came behind them and picked up the litter they'd left. So when he passed away, Mister Harriman left the ranch to the State of Idaho with the provision that it be posted flyfishing only.''

Like I said, I pass the story along as a fable, undocumented but undisputed. I do know that since hearing it I've gone a little farther out of my way to round up other people's empty containers and drink cans. As we hope and work for the establishment of more catch-and-release streams, our reputation as good outdoor citizens certainly won't hurt.

In the meantime, enjoy the fine trout fishing that Iowa has to offer.